Focused Mind

Sharpen Your Concentration To Achieve More

Ossama Khalaf

Book Cover by Kiryl Lysenka.

Illustrations by Dragan Milos.

First edition – 2025.

ISBN – 978-989-35979-0-3 (paperback).
ISBN – 978-989-35979-2-7 (hardcover).
ISBN – 978-989-35979-1-0 (ebook).

To the wandering minds seeking their way back to focus — may this book be your compass.

Contents

About this Book

This book is designed to take you on a systematic journey toward better focus, organized in five distinct parts that build upon each other.

Part I, "Focus Decoded," introduces core concepts and principles of concentration. Part II, "Focus Fractured," explores the various challenges that disrupt our attention in today's world. Part III, "Focus Redeemed," provides practical solutions and strategies to enhance your concentration. Part IV, "Focus Roadmap," helps you create a personalized plan to implement these insights into your daily life. Finally, Part V, "Focus Commandments," presents fundamental principles that remain relevant regardless of changes in technology, lifestyle, or circumstances.

Each chapter – within all parts - concludes with a "Putting It All Together" section that distills key takeaways. Following each part, you'll find a "Connecting the Dots" section that weaves together themes from all chapters in that part, helping you see the bigger picture and understand how different concepts interact.

Throughout the book, you'll encounter references to scientific research and expert insights that inform our understanding of focus. These correspond to detailed entries in the "End Notes" section, where you'll find not only full citations but also brief descriptions of key findings. This makes it easy to explore topics further or locate original sources for deeper study.

Think of this book as both a manual and a journey. You can read it straight through to build a comprehensive understanding, or use the clearly marked sections to focus on specific aspects of attention management that interest you most. Whether you're looking to understand why focus feels increasingly difficult, seeking practical strategies for better concentration, or ready to create a personalized focus improvement plan, you'll find what you need in these pages.

Let's begin your journey toward unwavering focus.

Introduction

Imagine yourself sitting at your desk, fully intending to tackle that important task you've been planning to finish today, only to be derailed by a barrage of distractions. Maybe you work in a busy research lab, surrounded by colleagues engaging in lively discussions or students popping in with questions about their running experiments. Or perhaps you work in a corporate office, where phones are constantly ringing and the hum of chatter fills the air. Even working from the comfort of your own home is not a refuge from distractions, as the responsibilities of family life can whisk you away from your work in an instant.

These scenarios are all too familiar to many of us. I'm sure we've all been there, struggling or even frustrated trying to maintain our focus in the face of countless distractions. It's as if our brains are being pulled in a dozen different directions, making it difficult to stay on track and get things done. But fear not, dear reader, you are not alone in this struggle. Over the years, I have had my own battles with distractions. I used to find myself scrambling to meet deadlines and stay on top of my workload. The constant interruptions and distractions seemed to chip away at my productivity, leaving me feeling frazzled and defeated.

It is from these personal struggles that the inspiration for this book emerged. Years of wrestling with the elusive nature of concentration have stirred me to take a step back and research the topic. What I discovered might surprise you: the average person loses nearly two hours of productive time each day to distractions. But here's the encouraging news – our ability to focus is not fixed. It's a skill we can develop, much like building a muscle. It was this revelation that motivated me to write this book. And so, "Focused Mind" was born, where I share the insights, strategies, and techniques I encountered on my journey to a better focus.

In these pages, you'll discover:

- Why your brain gets distracted (hint: it's not entirely your fault).
- Practical techniques that fit into your daily routine.
- Simple but powerful habits that can transform your productivity within weeks.

So, whether you're a researcher struggling to write that next paper, a corporate professional drowning in a sea of emails, or someone who simply wants to reclaim their attention span in this age of endless distractions, know that there is hope. Even if previous attempts to improve your focus have left you frustrated, the approach we'll explore together is different. It's backed up by science, and designed for the way we actually live and work today.

By embracing the principles outlined in this book and committing to the journey of self-improvement, you too can cultivate a focused mind capable of achieving greatness. Think of this book not as another self-help manual, but as a friendly guide to understanding and enhancing your natural ability to concentrate.

Here's to a future filled with clarity, productivity, and success. Buckle up, the ride is about to begin!

Enjoy,
Ossama

PART I

FOCUS DECODED

"Who Looks outside, dreams; Who looks inside, awakes."
-Carl Jung

The Inside Story

You know how some days you're completely in the zone, powering through tasks like a superhero, while other days you can't focus long enough to read a single email? In Part I, we're getting inside the fascinating world of focus, concentration, and attention – three mental powers that work together to help you achieve your goals. While many people use these terms interchangeably, they're more like close cousins than identical triplets. Each has its own unique role. Before we proceed, let's first understand what makes each one special:

Focus is your brain's spotlight, where everything else just fades into the background. It's like when you're at a concert, and the spotlight illuminates just one performer on stage. That's what focus does in your mind. It makes you zoom in on one specific thing, whether it's solving a puzzle, getting lost in a book, or listening to your friend's story about their weekend adventure.

Now, **concentration** is focus' endurance athlete friend. It's about keeping that spotlight steady for a long time, even when distractions try to steal the show. Think about when in a long meeting or studying for an exam without checking your phone every five minutes- that's concentration in action!

Attention, on the other hand, is the big picture player. It's your brain's way of sensing your environment, from the song playing in the background to the smell of coffee brewing. It's like a radar system in your brain constantly scanning everything around you and picking up on all sorts of information. For example, when you're crossing the street and notice an approaching car - that's your attention at work.

Here's the exciting part - these skills aren't set in stone. Your brain is like a muscle that can get stronger with practice. Scientists call this 'brain plasticity,' but I prefer to think of it as your brain's superpower to adapt and improve.

But wait, there's more! Focus isn't just about willpower. There are tiny chemical messengers in your brain called neurotransmitters working behind the scenes, like a backstage crew making sure everything runs smoothly. Your body's internal clock plays a crucial role too, determining your peak focus hours throughout the day.

Of course, focusing can be really tough for some of us, especially when having an attention disorder. But even with such attention challenges, there's hope! Understanding how your brain works is the first step to finding strategies that work for you.

In the upcoming chapters, we'll explore attention networks, brain plasticity, those chemical messengers, and how your body's natural rhythms affect your focus. Don't worry - while the science might sound complex, I promise to keep it engaging and practical.

I hear you saying what's the point? To help you understand your brain better so you can maximize your focus and concentration. After all, who couldn't use a mental upgrade in their daily life?

Ready? Let's get started!

1

Cognitive Tug-of-War

"You become what you give your attention to."
-Epictetus

Your Brain's Tag Team

Ever asked yourself how your brain knows what to focus on? It's quite remarkable - your brain actually comes with its own built-in spotlight system! Scientists have discovered special networks – something more of traffic controllers – that help you pay attention. They call these *attention networks,* and they work like a tag team: the *dorsal attention network* (or DAN) and the *ventral attention network* (or VAN). And since 'dorsal' means 'top or above' and 'ventral' means 'bottom or below' – this actually fits perfectly with how they work in our daily life!

Think of DAN as your brain's searchlight from *above*, actively looking for important things. When you decide to tackle something - like finishing a report before tomorrow's deadline - DAN kicks into gear. It helps you stay locked in on your task and filters out distractions like your neighbor's TV noise next-door. Ever been so deep in a book that you didn't hear someone calling your name? That's DAN doing its job!

Meanwhile, VAN is like your brain's built-in radar system from *below*, catching unexpected but important stuff that pops up around you. While DAN helps you focus, VAN keeps scanning your environment to catch unexpected but important stuff that pops up, and you might need to know about. Imagine you're deep in that report writing, fingers flying across the keyboard, when suddenly - BANG! A loud noise makes you jump. That's VAN giving you a nudge! Scientists also call it the 'salience network' because it spots things that stand out in your environment.

VAN might seem like a distraction machine, but it's actually crucial for our survival. Think about it this way: what if that loud bang was a fire alarm? Or your cat knocking over a vase? VAN's job is to make sure you don't miss anything crucial, even when you're completely absorbed in something else. Just like our cave-dwelling ancestors needed to notice a prowling predator while gathering food, today we need to hear that car horn when crossing the street while texting - though we shouldn't be doing that anyway, right?[1]

Great Balancing Act

Imagine your brain is hosting a party. DAN is your attentive party planner, keeping everything on schedule, while VAN is like your alert doorkeeper, watching for important arrivals or unexpected events.

---

1. Scientists describe how these networks function using two terms: 'top-down' processing, which is when DAN lets you consciously choose what to focus on - you're in the driver's seat; and 'bottom-up' processing, which is when VAN automatically alerts you to unexpected things in your environment, like sudden noises. Simply put, DAN lets you choose what gets your attention, while VAN lets your environment choose for you.

The cool part? These two networks are constantly working together. While DAN is helping you focus on decorating the perfect cake, VAN is still on lookout duty. If someone rings the doorbell, VAN checks with DAN, "Hey, should we open the door?" This is where it gets interesting. Your brain goes to the decision-maker[2], who steps in and help them decide if that doorbell is worth answering. Is it the pizza delivery guy? Better pause and attend to! Just a nosy neighbor? Back to the frosting!

It's a clever system, really. DAN keeps you focused on important tasks, while VAN makes sure you don't miss anything around you- which sometimes annoying, but other times it spots something really important, like when letting you know if your car is being towed outside. Handy, right? Like this, your brain is constantly balancing between being focused and staying aware, creating the perfect attention management team right inside your head.

Attention Headquarters

Now, let's see how this attention management team fits into your brain's bigger picture. These networks actually operate like a sophisticated company, where DAN and VAN are key department heads - working together in different 'offices'. DAN occupies the frontal and parietal regions, and VAN in the frontal and temporal regions. But above them sits your brain's CEO - the prefrontal cortex (PFC), overseeing everything and deciding what's worth your attention.

However, your PFC isn't just a simple decision-maker. It's more of a skilled conductor leading an orchestra, making sure everything runs smoothly. It handles several key executive functions (EF)[3] like:

---

2. That's the brain's CEO (aka prefrontal cortex).

3. Executive Functions (EF) are your brain's management tools - set of mental skills that help you get things done. They help you plan, focus, remember instructions, juggle multiple tasks, and filter out distractions.

- Setting goals and planning how to achieve them.
- Managing your attention by coordinating between DAN and VAN.
- Helping you resist distractions when you need to stay focused (i.e. impulse control).
- Allowing you to switch between tasks when necessary (i.e. cognitive flexibility).

But sometimes your brain's CEO can get overwhelmed, just like any busy executive can have an off day. When that happens, you might find it harder to focus or stay organized. It's like the conductor dropped their baton, and the orchestra is all out of sync! But here's the good news: just like a real CEO can improve their skills, your PFC can get better at its job too. How? By understanding how it works, you can learn ways to help it out and boost your brain power.

Attentional Gears

Now that we understand how your brain's attention team works together, let's look at the different ways they handle various cognitive challenges in your daily life. Scientists have identified three distinct ways your attention networks operate - they call these 'attentional modes' – like gears in your brain's attention machine.

The first gear is your selective attention - your brain's bouncer. It decides what gets into the VIP area of your mind and what doesn't. For example, when you're reading a book in a noisy café, your selective attention helps you focus on the words and tune out the chatter around you. Then in second gear, you have your sustained attention – your mental endurance athlete. When you need to concentrate on one task for a long time - like studying for an exam, or maybe binge-watching your favorite show - this mode keeps you going. And in third gear, you have your divided attention

- your inner juggler. This kicks in when you're multitasking, like cooking dinner while helping your kid with homework and listening to a podcast all at once. Showcasing these modes makes us appreciate how versatile our attention system really is - each mode perfectly suited for different situations we encounter throughout our day.

Putting It All Together

Now that you've learned about all of that, you might ask why you should care about all this brain stuff. Well, understanding the brain machinery behind attention explains so many everyday experiences, and can actually help you understand yourself better! Why you can focus easily in some places but in others you can't, or why concentration feels impossible when you're stressed or tired. It's not just about willpower - it's about complex networks working together to help you navigate your world.

Here's the exciting part: knowing how your attention system works is like reading the user manual of this part in your brain. Just as you can train your muscles at the gym, you can work with these networks to improve your focus. When you understand that DAN, VAN, and your PFC are doing their best to help you stay on track, you can be more patient with yourself on those days when focusing feels impossible.

Your attention system is incredibly sophisticated - it's not just about staying focused or getting distracted. It's about using the right attention gear for the right situation. So, next time you're struggling to concentrate, remember – you might just need a little help to shift to the right gear!

2
Shapeshifting Mind

"We are sculpting our brain with every thought."
-Rick Hanson

Your Plastic Fantastic Brain

Do you still remember Play-Doh? That silly putty from your childhood that you could stretch, mold, and bounce? Well, your brain is kind of like that, but way cooler. It's constantly reshaping itself based on what you do and think – a remarkable ability scientists call *brain plasticity*. Think of it as your brain's superpower to reorganize itself by forming new connections between its neurons (i.e. brain cells) throughout your life.

Want to see this brain-changing magic in action? Let's hop over to London and meet their taxi drivers. These cabbies face an incredibly tough test called "*The Knowledge*," where they must memorize every nook and cranny of London's complicated street system. To pass this exam, they need to know the most efficient routes between any two points in the city – no GPS allowed!

Here's where it gets fascinating: scientists discovered that experienced London cabbies actually developed larger posterior hippocampus (that's the brain's navigation center) compared to non-taxi drivers. It's as if their brains grew a better GPS system! This didn't happen randomly – it occurred because these drivers spent countless hours navigating London's maze-like streets on their mopeds. At first, they were constantly checking maps and getting lost, but over time, their brains adapted to meet this demanding challenge.

This example perfectly illustrates how brain plasticity isn't just about random changes – it's about your brain adapting to the specific demands you place on it. Your thoughts and actions are literally sculpting your brain, much like a sculptor shapes clay. Incredible, right?

Paying Attention: Brain's Workout Routine

Now, what's really interesting - your brain's ability to change (that Play-Doh-like quality) and your ability to focus are actually connected. Scientists call this relationship '*attentional plasticity*,' and it's pretty amazing. Think of it as a two-way street: paying attention changes your brain's physical structure by growing new connections between neurons, and these changes help you get even better at focusing over time.

It's like your brain is a musician, and paying attention is its instrument. The more your brain practices, the better it gets at playing that focus tune. Remember the last time you started a new book? At first, your mind probably wandered after just a few pages. But as you kept at it, forcing yourself to continue reading, something magical happened. Suddenly, you could focus longer, zip through pages, and get completely absorbed in the story. That wasn't just coincidence – it was your brain adapting and improving its focus skills through attentional plasticity!

Research backs this up showing that people who practice intense concentration– not just going through the motions, but really engaging with what they're doing – actually reshape their brain's attention networks. It's like going to a mental gym where your attention muscles get stronger with each workout! Scientists have found that even short periods of focused "*attention training*" can lead to noticeable improvements in cognitive performance. These aren't just subjective improvements– researchers could actually measure these changes in the brain[1] .

Use It or Lose It

Just like a muscle, your focus can actually get better or worse – it all depends on how you use your brain. Let me share a compelling study about video gamers. Scientists discovered that regular gamers had more grey matter[2] in their prefrontal cortex – remember, that's the brain's CEO for attention and decision-making.

Think of your brain as a super-advanced computer, with that grey matter being the processor that handles all the heavy lifting for thinking, remembering, and making decisions. When scientists talk about having more grey matter in an area, they're basically saying that part of your brain has more '*processing power*.' So these gamers, just by playing games that required focus and quick decisions, were unknowingly giving their prefrontal cortex a serious workout – upgrading their attention processor without even realizing it!

---

1. Attention training - the practice of deliberate, sustained focus while resisting distractions - can enhance your brain's attention networks. In 2013, a study found that participants showed improved working memory and reading comprehension after just couple of weeks of training, with measurable changes in brain activity.

2. It's called 'grey' because it looks greyish-pink in real life (not that you'd want to see it!).

But here's the thing – it's not just about video games. This shows that **whatever you spend hours of your time doing shapes your brain**. If you practice focusing, your brain gets better at it. On the flip side, if you're always distracted... well, your brain might get too good at being distracted!

Putting It All Together

The science of brain plasticity sends you an incredibly empowering message: your brain is constantly changing in response to your experiences and habits. Just like those London taxi drivers' brains adapted to become navigation experts, your brain can transform into a focus champion – no matter where you're starting from!

The dynamic relationship between plasticity and attention explains those day-to-day focus fluctuations, and why consistent mental habits can create lasting improvements in your concentration. Think of your focus as a brain muscle that needs training. Each mental workout adds up, making your brain stronger and more efficient at paying attention. And just like with physical exercise, consistency is key. You wouldn't expect to bench press 200 pounds on your first day at the gym, right? The same goes for your brain – improvement comes with **regular**, **intentional** practice.

The takeaway? You're not stuck with the attention span you have today. So next time someone tells you that you can't improve your focus, you can tell them that science says otherwise! Now that you know your brain is ready and willing to change, the question is: are you ready to start sculpting your super-focused brain?

3

Focus Modulators

"Neurotransmitters - the brain's chemical guardians, each shaping our feelings and behaviors."
-Ossama Khalaf

Your Brain's All-Star Team

Imagine your brain as a bustling city, with neurons as the citizens. How do these citizens talk to each other? That's where neurotransmitters come in – they're like the text messages of your brain. Picture your neurons having their own WhatsApp group for communication!

These tiny chemical messengers are the words your brain uses to express your feelings and behaviors. They influence your ability to focus, concentrate, and pretty much everything else your brain does. Curious to meet some of the stars of your brain's focus team?

Dopamine: Your Cheerleader

First up is dopamine (DA), and it's not just about pleasure (though it definitely plays a role there). Think of it as a tiny cheerleader in your brain, always ready with a motivational chant. It's there to get you pumped up to pursue goals and stay focused on tasks.

Scientists discovered that in your brain's attentional headquarters – your PFC – dopamine helps filter out distractions. The equivalent of having a personal assistant saying, "Hey! Keep your eye on that important thing!" when you're tempted to check your phone instead of finishing your work. So, if you ever been so engrossed in a task that you completely lost track of time, then you've experienced dopamine working its magic.

But dopamine also plays a part in your brain's reward system, and will make you feel good once you accomplish a task. Remember that awesome feeling after a good workout or a focused work session? That's your brain sending dopamine to give you a high-five for a job well done! And every time you sustain your attention on something, you get this dopamine boost. Such shot of dopamine acts like the perfect energy drink for your concentration, fueling your motivation to stay focused.

There's just one catch – you need to find the right dopamine levels to keep you going. It's like adjusting the volume on your music player: too low, and you can't hear the music (low motivation, trouble focusing); too loud, and it's overwhelming (over-excitement, or getting anxious). But when it's just right, you can enjoy the music perfectly (the right dopamine dose for optimal focus)!

Norepinephrine: Your Coach

Next up is norepinephrine (NE). If dopamine is the cheerleader, then norepinephrine is the coach with the loudest whistle in town! It's your alarm clock –the one that shakes your attention to wake up when you need it most. One blow from the coach's whistle and you're immediately on your toes, ready in your gear. Remember that time you were slacking, but had a tight deadline and all of a sudden found the clarity to finish your work? That was a norepinephrine kick!

Science shows that NE ensures you're alert and ready to react, especially when you're stressed or excited. NE is part of the brain's emergency response team, always on standby. When this coach blows the whistle and yells, "Hey! This is important! Pay attention!" your brain snaps into action, sharp and focused, ready to make quick decisions about what really matters.

Acetylcholine: Your Librarian

Meet acetylcholine (ACh), another superstar on your brain's focus team. If your brain is a big library, ACh would be the expert librarian there. Just like a good librarian helps you find books, stay focused on your reading, and remember where to return them, ACh manages your attention and memory.

This librarian has two key responsibilities. First, it helps you concentrate on what you're learning – like staying focused when you're picking up a new language. Second, it makes sure that information gets properly filed away in your memory banks. It's the difference between just reading something and actually remembering it later. So, this master organizer keeps your mental library running efficiently, helping you both focus on what's important now and store it away for later use.

ACh is also crucial for your "*attentional effort*" – that extra mental push you need when things get tough. Imagine you're studying late at night or sitting through a long meeting. Even though you're tired, ACh helps you maintain focus by turning up the brightness of your brain's spotlight. It's like having a librarian who whispers, "I know you're tired, but let's stay with this chapter just a bit longer because it's important."

Serotonin: Your Mood Technician

Serotonin (5-HT), often known as the "feel-good" chemical, does more than just boost your mood – it could be considered your brain's lighting technician, setting the perfect atmosphere for your mind to work at its best. Just as good lighting can make everything in a room look clearer and feel better, serotonin helps fine-tune your attention.

Research shows that the right levels of serotonin improve your *cognitive flexibility* – your ability to smoothly switch between tasks. As if this lighting operator in your brain is adept at swiftly directing your attention where it needs to go, tuning your brain's attention networks (the DAN - "focus on this" and VAN - "watch out for that" – remember?) work together seamlessly. The result? You can focus longer and switch between tasks without getting mentally tangled up.

GABA & Glutamate: Your Yin & Yang

Last but not least, meet GABA and Glutamate – your brain's Yin and Yang. Think of them as two instructors with very different teaching styles, working together to create the perfect balance in your brain.

GABA is your brain's chill-out specialist, like that serene yoga instructor who can make you feel Zen even on your most stressful days. When GABA's in charge, it's all about taking it easy and unwinding. Meanwhile, Glutamate is your animated fitness trainer, always ready to get things moving and keep your brain fired up. When Glutamate's in charge, it's all about action and excitement.

Your brain needs both these opposite forces working in harmony – it's all about finding that sweet spot between Netflix-and-chill and doing burpees! When GABA and Glutamate are perfectly balanced, you hit that ideal state: alert but not stressed, focused but not frazzled. It's like having just the right mix of rest and activity in your day – productive yet peaceful and relaxed.

Putting It All Together

All of your neurotransmitters participate in a perfectly choreographed dance. There's no solo star here – it's all about teamwork. Your cheerleader dopamine keeps spirits high, coach norepinephrine maintains alertness, librarian acetylcholine manages information flow, mood technician serotonin sets the right atmosphere, and the GABA-glutamate duo maintains perfect balance.

When they're all in sync, performing their chemical ballet, that's when you experience laser-sharp focus and unwavering concentration. But if the rhythm is off, you might find yourself struggling with scattered thoughts until the team finds its groove again.

Keep in mind that we've just scratched the surface of the neurotransmitter world. Scientists are constantly discovering more about these remarkable brain chemicals. While you can't directly control that neural troupe, understanding its members helps you appreciate the incredible complexity behind your ability to focus – and the amazing potential of your own brain.

4

Internal Timekeeper

"The whole universe is built on rhythms. Everything happens in circles, in spirals." -John Hartford

Your Body's Clock Network

Ever wonder why your brain feels like it's on fire at certain times of day, while at others you're reaching for that third cup of coffee? Welcome to the charming world of circadian rhythm – your body's internal timekeeper that orchestrates everything from your attention span to your energy levels.

Remember how we pictured your brain as a bustling city with its citizen neurons sending messages to each other? Well, let's zoom out to see an even bigger picture. That city isn't just bustling – it's a sophisticated metropolis with its own advanced time management system. At its heart sits the suprachiasmatic nucleus (SCN), a control center no bigger than a grain of rice, acting like city hall's master clock. This tiny timekeeper monitors environmental cues like sunlight and temperature to keep the whole metropolis running on schedule.

What's remarkable is that your body's timekeeping isn't limited to this central clock. You could view it as a network of synchronized time zones across different city districts. While city hall's clock (the SCN) sets the official time, each district (different organs) also has its own clock, fine-tuning local activities while staying coordinated with the central time. It's like each neighborhood adapting its rhythm to local needs while still keeping in step with the city's master schedule.

Zeitgebers

So, what keeps your body's master clock running on time? While the SCN acts as city hall's timekeeper, it doesn't work alone. Just like a modern city relies on various signals to coordinate its activities, your body's timing system responds to special cues or signals called "*zeitgebers*" (a German word meaning "time givers"). These time cues help to align all internal operations with the outside world.

Those time signals help your internal clock stay in sync through a process called "*entrainment.*" It's like how a city needs to adjust its operations when daylight saving time kicks in – all the districts need to reset their schedules accordingly. Without these external cues, your internal clock might drift, running slightly longer or shorter than 24 hours. You've probably experienced this during jet lag, when your body's city needs time to adjust to a new time zone.

Your body's metropolis is constantly monitoring these time signals to fine-tune its daily rhythm. While some zeitgebers are social (like your daily routines and interactions), the most powerful one is sunlight – it's the official time signal that all city operations rely on. From the morning light that signals to your body it's time to wake up, to the evening routines that prepare you for bedtime, these time signals play a part in tuning the beat of your body's daily biological rhythms. So, let's explore these different time signals and how they influence your attention and focus throughout the day.

Light - The Master Signal

First off, the star of the show - light. Just as a city comes alive with the sunrise, your body's metropolis takes its primary cues from light. Your central clock has light sensors throughout the city, constantly monitoring daylight levels to keep all operations running on schedule. Research shows that bright light exposure can boost both alertness and mental performance – that's why working near a window or taking a quick outdoor break can help refresh your focus.

Interestingly, not everyone's internal clock ticks to the same schedule. Some are "larks" (morning people) who are ready for action at dawn. While others are "owls" (evening people) who hit their peak when the sun goes down. Most of us fall somewhere between these extremes, with our own unique peak hours. Scientists call these personal timing preferences "*chronotypes*," and they play a big role in determining when your mental performance is at its best.

Sleep – Reset Time

Next up is something we all love but often don't get enough of - sleep! You know how you feel foggy and can't seem to concentrate after a late night? Well, there's a good reason for that. Let me explain what's happening in your body's metropolis after hours.

Your brain during the day is like the city's business district - bustling with activity, information flying everywhere like papers in a busy office. But when night falls, something remarkable happens. While you are sleeping, there's an essential crew of night janitors come into action. Their job isn't just about turning off the lights for your brain to rest - they're busy organizing the day's information, filing away memories, clearing out mental clutter, and reseting all systems for tomorrow's operations.

When you cut your sleep short, it's like giving this maintenance crew only half their shift to complete their work. The result? Your city's operations suffer the next day. Research shows even mild sleep deprivation can shrink your attention span and muddle your memory - it's hard to run a city efficiently when yesterday's work is still scattered everywhere!

Meal O'clock

Just when you thought your internal timing system couldn't get more complex - enter your stomach's clock! Like other districts in your body's metropolis, your digestive system runs on its own precise schedule, coordinating with the central timekeeper.

Your stomach is not your body's food processor, it's more of a food distribution hub, with carefully planned delivery schedules. Research shows it's not just what food is being delivered, but when it is delivered can affect your cognitive performance. Scientists discovered this by having people shift their meal times by 5 hours later than usual for few days – to find that there is a 5-hour shift in their body's "glucose rhythms" – their glucose management system. Such important biological process changed its schedule to match the new meal schedule the participant followed in the study.

Why does this matter for your ability to focus? Imagine your brain is expecting an energy delivery at noon every day – your usual lunchtime. Suddenly switch that delivery to 5 PM, and you've got essential mental operations running low on fuel when it needs it most. During this schedule adjustment, your attention might waver as your brain is still confused and tries to figure out the new delivery timetable.

This isn't just about managing hunger - your meal timing actually sends important time signals to the rest of your body. Disrupt these signals, and you might find your focus taking some time off! So, when planning your meals, remember: you're not just feeding your belly, you're tuning up your attention span too!

Social Schedule

Every one of us has a natural rhythm and a socially-imposed one. Imagine your body's metropolis operating on one time zone while the outside world demands it to function in another - that's what we call '*social jetlag*.'

Think about it: your body might naturally power down at midnight and restart at 8 AM, but society (your job) requires operations to begin at 6 AM. During the workweek, you're forcing your body to run on an unnatural schedule. Then comes the weekend, and your body tries to return to its preferred timing - like a weekly mini jet lag. No wonder Mondays feel so rough - your body's constantly switching between two different time zones trying to readjust to the early schedule again. Such social jetlag will make you feel groggy, and inattentive.

Your body takes timing cues from various daily activities:

- *Community Gatherings*: Regular dinners with family or friends aren't just for bonding - they help synchronize your body's clock.

- *Regular Appointments*: That weekly yoga class or book club you attend every Tuesday – it does more than enriching your life - it provides consistent time signals.

- *Evening Screen Time*: Those late-night scrolling sessions are like keeping your city's lights blazing when it needs to wind down. It messes with the production of your sleep hormone (melatonin) and will leave you foggy the next morning.

- *Exercise Timing*: When to workout matters too. A morning jog might wake up your brain in different ways than an evening gym session.

These activities act like little signals to your body, helping it know what time it is and what it should be doing- when they're consistent, your body's clock runs smoothly, and you're more likely to feel alert and focused when you need to be. But when these signals get scrambled, you might struggle to maintain peak performance.

So, next time you're planning your day, remember: your body is constantly paying attention to these social time signals, even if you don't notice them. The better aligned these signals are with your natural rhythm, the more efficiently your body runs!

Neurotransmitter Rhythm

Remember those neurotransmitters - your city's chemical messengers? Turns out they don't just randomly zip around your brain's metropolis. They follow their own precise delivery schedules, especially dopamine, your focus cheerleader!

Scientists discovered that dopamine isn't like a 24/7 gas station providing fuel whenever needed. Instead, think of it as a scheduled delivery service, making its rounds at specific times throughout the day. Research shows these deliveries peak and dip at different hours, creating what we might call your city's "focus fuel schedule."

What does this mean for your daily operations? Just as a city has rush hours and quiet periods, your brain has prime times for concentration. These are the hours when your dopamine delivery service is running at full capacity, making it easier to focus and get things done. Just as you might plan your commute around traffic patterns, you could schedule your most demanding tasks around your brain's natural "fuel delivery" peaks!

But here's the thing - everyone's internal clock is a bit different. Your personal "focus fuel" schedule might not be exactly the same as your friend's or coworker's. The key is to pay attention to when you naturally feel most alert and focused - that might be your brain's dopamine happy hour!

Putting It All Together

Your body's metropolis runs on an intricate network of timekeepers, from the master clock at city hall (SCN) to the local time zones in each district. Just like a well-run city, your body relies on various signals - from sunlight and sleep to meals and social activities - to keep all its operations synchronized.

Understanding these rhythms isn't about forcing your city to run on someone else's schedule. Instead, it's about recognizing your own natural patterns and working with them. When do you naturally feel most alert? When does your dopamine delivery service run most efficiently? These are your body's hints about when to schedule your most attention-demanding tasks.

Everyone's rhythm is special. Some are highly sensitive to external signals, while others march to their own beat. The key is to listen to your body, respect its natural cycles, and harmonize your activities with your unique biological beat.

5

Mind Mischief

"Mental illness is not a personal failure, it is in the way we have responded to people with mental disorders."
-Gro Harlem Brundtland

Different Minds, Different Challenges

We have explored how our brain normally manages attention, like a well-run city with its traffic signals and control systems working in harmony. But what happens when these systems start behaving differently? Sometimes, our brain's management systems can get overwhelmed, send mixed signals, or process information in unexpected ways.

In this chapter, we'll explore how conditions like ADHD, depression, anxiety, and others influence our ability to concentrate and manage attention. But here's the important bit – this isn't just about understanding what goes wrong. It's about appreciating the incredible diversity in how different minds process information and manage attention. Some minds might need alternative ways to handle challenges, while others might require different approaches to maintaining focus.

ADHD - The Next Shiny Thing

First up on our tour of attention challenges is Attention Deficit Hyperactivity Disorder (ADHD)[1] . Imagine your brain is a curious puppy in a park full of squirrels - that's what ADHD feels like! The brain is wired for excitement, always on the lookout for the next shiny thing - something new and interesting.

For someone with ADHD, the world is filled with interesting "squirrels" or "shiny objects"- each representing a new thought, idea, or stimulus. Every movement, or sound is impossible to ignore, and there's a constant urge to check for something new and exciting. Studies show that their brains have structural differences, particularly in regions controlling attention. Their attention isn't broken - it's more like a butterfly, always flitting to the next colorful flower - explaining why someone might start a task with enthusiasm but struggle to stick with it. Their impulse control (the brain's brake pedal) as well isn't as strong, making it harder to stop chasing every squirrel.

However, here's where it gets interesting - sometimes people with ADHD can 'hyperfocus' on engaging tasks. It's like finally catching that squirrel, and nothing else in the world exists. This intense focus can lead to incredible productivity and creativity... until something else catches their attention.

---

1. ADHD is a neurodevelopmental condition characterized by persistent patterns of inattention, hyperactivity, and impulsivity that affect daily functioning and development.

Understanding all that about ADHD helps us see that distractibility isn't a choice - it's how the brain is wired. The ability to hyperfocus shows that it's not about an inability to concentrate, but rather a different way of processing attention. While navigating a squirrel-filled park every day can be challenging, with the right strategies, people with ADHD can harness their unique way of thinking to achieve remarkable things.

Depression - Through the Fog

Next comes depression[2] and its effect on attention - what many people describe as "brain fog." This isn't just a metaphor; imagine your mind on a clear, sunny day, then watch as a thick, heavy fog rolls in, making everything harder to see and reach.

Depression turns your brain's processing speed to low battery mode – everything takes longer to understand and accomplish. Your sharp thinking feels dulled. It's challenging to focus - you might read the same sentence repeatedly, struggle to follow conversations, or lose your train of thought mid-sentence. Even your memory gets affected – appointments slip away, familiar information becomes hard to recall, and organizing your thoughts is tough.

Research shows these cognitive challenges aren't just subjective experiences – they're measurable effects of depression on brain function. The fog affects everything from simple tasks to complex problem-solving, making each mental effort feel like pushing through a heavy resistance.

Living with depression isn't just about feeling sad; it's like navigating life through a foggy windshield. Everything requires more effort and concentration. While some symptoms may improve with treatment, cognitive difficulties might take time to clear. However, recognizing these

2. Depression is a mental health disorder characterized by persistent feelings of sadness, hopelessness, and loss of interest in activities. It's more than just feeling down; it's like carrying a heavy emotional weight that affects your thoughts, feelings, and behaviors, often making everyday tasks feel overwhelming.

challenges is often the first step toward finding ways to work through the fog.

Anxiety – Constant Alert Mode

Anxiety is another condition that can significantly mess with your focus. Imagine trying to concentrate while your brain persistently shouts "What if?" It's like being stuck in a mental tug-of-war between what you need to focus on and an endless stream of worries competing for your attention.

Usually the built-in attention spotlight in our brains is something most people can easily direct – to focus on your homework, your favorite TV show, or that book you're reading. However, when anxiety takes hold, this spotlight develops a mind of its own. Instead of focusing on what you want, your mind constantly switches to worry about potential threats. Research shows that anxiety puts your brain into "threat detection mode" – to become incredibly quick at noticing potential threats. You might be the first to spot a subtle change in someone's tone or sense that something's slightly off. However, this heightened awareness comes at a cost – trying to read a book or follow a conversation becomes challenging when your mind keeps interrupting with "Did I leave the stove on?" or "What if I fail tomorrow's test?"

While anxiety doesn't necessarily make you less effective at tasks – you might still complete them – it does make your brain work much harder to achieve the same results. It's like driving with one foot on the brake: you'll reach your destination, but you'll use much more energy getting there. Understanding this helps explain why anxiety isn't just about feeling worried – it's about your brain's attention system working overtime to keep you safe, even when you'd rather it focus elsewhere.

OCD - Stuck on Loop

Obsessive-Compulsive Disorder (OCD)[3] has a unique way of hijacking attention. Imagine a mind with an overzealous emergency system that keeps triggering false alarms. While others can easily verify and dismiss these alerts as unnecessary, someone with OCD can't simply turn them off, even when they know there's no real danger.

For someone with OCD, intrusive thoughts (obsessions) flood the mind like urgent emergency broadcasts. Even when you're trying to focus on a task, these alerts keep tapping you on the shoulder demanding immediate attention. To manage these thoughts, people feel compelled to perform certain actions or mental rituals – like having an insistent GPS that keeps rerouting you down the same paths, even when you know they're not the most efficient routes to your destination.

Research shows that this constant battle between focusing on daily tasks and responding to OCD's demands creates unique challenges. It's exhausting, like trying to remember a phone number while someone's shouting random words at you. Task-switching becomes particularly difficult – once the warning system activates, it's hard to redirect attention elsewhere. While some people with OCD might develop enhanced attention to detail, this can become a double-edged sword, making it harder to see the big picture or complete tasks efficiently.

Think of someone trying to write a simple email but getting stuck in an endless loop of re-reading and editing because of intrusive thoughts about potential misunderstandings, or starting to clean their room but spending hours organizing one drawer because their mind keeps insisting it's not quite right. Understanding these patterns helps us see that OCD isn't

---

3. OCD is a mental health condition characterized by persistent, intrusive thoughts (obsessions) and repetitive behaviors or mental acts (compulsions) that a person feels compelled to perform in response to these thoughts. It's like having a stuck record player in your mind, repeatedly playing worries or fears, and feeling an intense need to perform certain actions to quiet these thoughts. These patterns significantly impact daily functioning and attention.

about being picky or perfectionist – it's about a mind caught in a cycle of intrusive thoughts and compulsive responses.

Autism - Enhanced Perception

For people on the autism spectrum[4], attention operates like a uniquely powerful spotlight. When this spotlight lands on something interesting, it doesn't just illuminate – it reveals every detail with extraordinary clarity, as if viewing the world in ultra-high definition.

This attention system has remarkable capabilities. Research suggests people with autism can process more information simultaneously than others – imagine being able to see every leaf on a tree distinctly rather than just the overall shape. This enhanced perception often translates into an incredible eye for detail and patterns that others might miss entirely. However, this same ability can make busy environments overwhelming, as every sensory input demands full attention.

The autistic spotlight also tends to be "sticky" – once focused on something engaging, it can be difficult to redirect. A person might become deeply absorbed in learning everything about dinosaurs or mastering a particular skill, showing remarkable expertise and focus. Yet switching to a different topic or task can be challenging, as if the spotlight needs extra time and effort to move to a new target.

This unique way of processing information extends to how social and environmental cues are perceived. While most people's attention naturally gravitates toward faces and social interactions, someone with autism might focus more on objects or environmental details. Think of an adult who excels at detail-oriented work but finds open-plan offices challenging due

---

4. Autism, or Autism Spectrum Disorder (ASD), is a neurodevelopmental condition characterized by differences in social communication, sensory processing, and patterns of behavior or interests. It represents a unique way of perceiving and interacting with the world, with each person on the spectrum having a unique combination of strengths and challenges.

to the constant stream of sensory information that others might easily filter out.

Understanding this high-definition way of experiencing the world helps us appreciate that autism isn't about deficits in attention – it's about a mind that processes information with exceptional clarity and detail, even if that sometimes means needing different ways to manage the abundance of information.

Bipolar Disorder - Attention Rollercoaster

Bipolar disorder[5] creates a unique rollercoaster effect on attention. Think of your focus like a car on a track with dramatic highs (mania) and lows (depression), each potentially lasting for weeks or months. It's as if your mind's energy settings keep switching between turbo mode and power saving, with each shift significantly affecting how you process information and maintain attention.

During manic highs, it's like your attention car has hit an exhilarating downhill stretch. Everything becomes faster and more intense – thoughts race at lightning speed, and you might feel capable of focusing on countless things simultaneously. Projects get started with incredible enthusiasm, and you could work for hours without feeling tired. However, during depressive lows, that same car feels like it's struggling up a steep hill. Everything slows down, concentration becomes foggy, and even simple tasks feel overwhelming.

Research shows that even during stable periods (an in-between period called "*euthymia*" - a normal, tranquil mental state or mood), attention can still fluctuate. It's like your car is on a flat stretch of track, but the engine isn't running quite smoothly. You might find it harder to maintain focus

---

5. Bipolar disorder is a mental health condition characterized by dramatic shifts in the "emotional thermostat" between two extremes - emotional highs (mania) and lows (depression), affecting energy levels, thinking patterns, and attention capacity.

or filter out distractions. Like a computer with background programs constantly running – even when the mood stabilizes, these programs can still affect how efficiently your "attention software" operates.

Learning to navigate this attention rollercoaster becomes crucial – like becoming an expert at handling a vehicle through various track conditions. During high-energy periods, it's about channeling that intense focus productively. In low periods, it means breaking tasks into manageable pieces. And during stable times, it's about developing strategies to maintain steady attention despite the lingering effects. Understanding these patterns helps explain why attention changes aren't a personal failing, but rather a natural part of how bipolar disorder affects the mind's processing system.

The Common Connection

To appreciate the gravity of these clinical conditions, a comprehensive study across these attention challenges revealed a fascinating pattern: they all affect executive function – your brain's management tools – in unique ways. It's like each condition creates its own specific disruption in this essential management system. Here's how:

- ADHD scrambles the multitasking system, making it difficult to juggle tasks or switch between them smoothly.

- Depression slows down the planning department, making it harder to map out steps toward goals.

- OCD overloads the behavioral control unit, making it difficult to stop repetitive thoughts or actions.

- Anxiety floods the working memory office with worried thoughts, making it hard to hold onto important information.

- Autism affects the flexibility unit, making unexpected changes especially challenging.

- Bipolar disorder impacts the emotional control system, causing it to fluctuate between extremes.

Understanding this common thread helps explain something important: while these conditions might look similar from the outside – perhaps as general difficulties with organization or focus – they each affect the brain's management center in distinct ways. This insight does more than just explain similar-looking struggles; it helps us understand that these challenges stem from real differences in how the brain's management system operates, not from lack of effort or willpower.

Putting It All Together

Our journey through different attention patterns reveals something remarkable: each mind has its own unique way of processing information and managing focus. Some minds notice every detail with crystal clarity, others juggle multiple thoughts simultaneously, and some experience dramatic shifts in their attention patterns.

These differences aren't flaws – they're variations in how our brains operate. Just as each person develops their own ways of navigating life's challenges, each mind creates unique strategies for managing attention. There's no such thing as a 'standard' way of focusing - what matters is understanding how your particular mind works and learning to work with its own distinct attention span.

Remember, if your attention works differently from others, you're part of the rich diversity of human cognition, each pattern bringing its own strengths and challenges. In the upcoming chapters, we'll explore practical strategies to help your unique mind thrive, regardless of how it processes information or manages attention.

Connecting the Dots

Symphony of Focus

Let's pause to marvel at how our brain's focus system works like a complex but beautiful symphony. Each element we've explored contributes its own unique part to this remarkable performance of focus.

Attention Headquarters

Remember our dynamic duo, DAN and VAN? The brain's attention controllers, with DAN helping you zoom in on important tasks while VAN keeps watch for unexpected but important events. But they don't work alone – they're guided by your prefrontal cortex, the skilled conductor that coordinates attention shifts and helps resist distractions.

Power to Change

Thanks to brain plasticity, this entire system is constantly fine-tuning itself. Like an orchestra in rehearsal, your brain gets better with each practice session. Just as London's taxi drivers developed better navigation centers through experience, your focus networks can strengthen through consistent use. It's not about trying harder – it's about giving your brain regular opportunities to practice and build stronger attention pathways.

Chemical Dance

Your neurotransmitters play essential roles in this performance: dopamine cheers you on and rewards your effort, norepinephrine keeps you alert, acetylcholine helps you process and remember information, serotonin helps you switch between tasks smoothly, while GABA and glutamate maintain the perfect balance between calm and excitement.

Daily Rhythm

All of these systems follow your body's internal clock which conducts this performance according to its own schedule. Your focus normally ebbs and flows throughout the day. Understanding the natural circadian patterns – from your peak alertness hours to how sleep, meals, and daily routines affect your attention – helps you know when your brain is primed to focus and when it needs rest.

Unique Patterns

Sometimes these systems work differently, as we've seen with various attention challenges. But whether your mind processes information in high definition, operates at varying speeds, or tends to notice everything at once, understanding these patterns helps you develop strategies that work with your unique brain wiring.

Grand Performance

When all these elements work together – attention networks directing traffic, brain plasticity creating stronger pathways, neurotransmitters delivering their perfectly timed messages, and circadian rhythms conducting the daily schedule – we witness the remarkable symphony of focus. Each system plays its crucial part, from the vigilant VAN watching for unexpected solos to dopamine's encouraging cheer keeping the momentum going.

Understanding this interplay helps us appreciate this complex biological orchestra, and why focus isn't simply about trying harder. Some days concentration comes easily; other days, your brain needs more time to find its rhythm. Both experiences are natural parts of how our cognitive systems function. So, remember to be patient with yourself when focus feels elusive.

As we move forward, we'll explore practical strategies to work with your brain's natural tendencies rather than fighting against them. After all, the goal isn't to force yourself into someone else's pattern – it's to understand and enhance your own distinct way of focusing.

PART II

FOCUS FRACTURED

"The ability to focus is becoming the scarcest commodity of the 21st century." -Cal Newport

Ecosystem Under Siege

Einstein once said, "In the middle of difficulty lies opportunity." When it comes to our fractured focus in today's world, these words ring especially true. Your scattered attention isn't just a problem to solve – it's an invitation to understand and strengthen your mind's capabilities.

Think of your focus as a delicate ecosystem, where concentration ebbs and flows based on countless internal and external influences. In this part of our journey, we'll explore five major forces that can disturb this fragile balance, each capable of fracturing your attention in unique ways.

Picture your daily focus under siege: distractions bombard like constant rainfall, habits grow like persistent vegetation, energy levels rise and fall like tides, stress sweeps through like sudden storms, and emotions color everything like changing seasons. Each of these forces plays a crucial role in determining whether your mental ecosystem thrives or struggles.

In the chapters ahead, we'll examine:

- The true cost of constant interruptions on your attention.
- How habits either support or drain your focus.
- Why energy levels alter your ability to concentrate.
- How stress scatters your thoughts like leaves in a storm.
- The way your emotional landscape colors everything you try to accomplish.

Understanding these disruptive forces isn't just about identifying problems – it's about recognizing how your focus ecosystem responds to different challenges. Think of this section as your field guide to concentration: by understanding what fractures your focus, you take the first step toward protecting it.

Ready to explore what really fractures your mental ecosystem?

6
Distraction Overload

"The greatest enemy to progress is not stagnation, but distraction." -Tony Robbins

Just Another Workday

You're in the zone, fingers flying across the keyboard, ideas flowing smoothly, and then – ping! There goes your email notification, breaking your perfect flow state[1] . "Just a quick check," you tell yourself. But that seemingly innocent interruption is like a pebble dropped in a calm pond

1. The mental state of complete immersion and focused concentration where work feels effortless.

– the ripples spread until your entire workday is churning with lost focus, mounting stress, and endless catch-up work. Sound familiar?

If you're nodding along thinking, "That's exactly my day!" - you're not alone. In our modern workplaces, distractions are as common as coffee mugs on desks. And while we might brush them off as minor annoyances, these interruptions affect our work and well-being more deeply than we realize. In this chapter, we'll peek into typical workplaces to unmask the sneaky villains lurking there. We'll explore how these interruptions secretly sabotage your productivity, and why that "quick email check" costs far more than just the few seconds it takes to read it.

Distraction Spectrum

Technically, interruptions and distractions are related but slightly different. An interruption is when you have to completely stop what you're doing, like putting down your book when someone calls your name. A distraction, on the other hand, is more like reading that book with the TV on in the background – you're still reading, but not as effectively.

For our purposes, though, we'll treat them as partners in crime. Whether it's a major interruption that pulls you away entirely or a minor distraction that just divides your attention, the end result is the same: you're not operating at your best.

But we're not all in the same boat when it comes to dealing with interruptions. Just like some people can sleep through a rock concert while others wake up at a whisper, our vulnerability to distractions largely depends on our work type and the mental effort it requires:

Focus-Intensive Work

Tasks that demand constant cognitive engagement – like complex problem-solving, creative writing, or detailed analysis. If you're a knowledge worker – like a scientist, engineer, or writer – your productivity depends heavily on your ability to concentrate deeply on complex tasks. For you, distractions can be particularly costly, disrupting the delicate mental processes needed for the task.

Light-Processing Work

Tasks that don't require full mental engagement, like data entry, organizing files or following routine procedures. Manual workers – like farmers, mechanics, construction workers – often engage in these activities. While still requiring skill and attention, they're more resistant to distractions because they rely on well-practiced physical actions. Interruptions can still slow them down, but their impact isn't quite as severe because these tasks are easier to pick up quickly after a disruption.

However, it's not about your job title as most jobs involve both types of work. A mechanic might spend most time on routine repairs (light-processing) but switch to focus-intensive work when diagnosing an unusual problem. Similarly, a scientist might alternate between deep analysis (focus-intensive) and routine data entry (light-processing). The key factor is how much mental bandwidth your current task demands. Understanding this spectrum helps explain why some days distractions bounce right off you, while other times they seem impossible to ignore.

In the coming sections, we'll explore two main categories of distractions: those that come from within our own minds and those that ambush us from our environment. We'll see how they affect our work, and why some are harder to ignore than others.

When Your Biggest Distractor Is... You!

Sometimes the most challenging distractions come from within our own minds. Unlike external interruptions- a ringing phone or chatty colleague that you can sometimes avoid, these internal distractors are particularly tricky because they're part of how our brains naturally work.

Mental Meanderings

Research shows that up to 47% of people experience mind wandering[2], and we could spend up to 30% of our waking hours lost in it. That's right – almost one-third of your day could be an unplanned mental vacation! One moment you're working on a report, the next you're thinking about weekend plans or replaying a conversation from yesterday. These unplanned mental detours can significantly impact your productivity, especially during focus-intensive tasks. The participants of this study reported that it seriously affected their concentration on what they were trying to do.

Daydreaming[3] deserves special attention because while it can spark creativity and enhance problem-solving, frequent uncontrolled daydreaming can seriously impact your productivity. It's like having an imaginative child in your head – full of wonderful ideas but not great at sitting still when there's work to be done. The challenge lies in managing this mental activity when you need to concentrate on immediate tasks.

Mind Chatter

That's what scientists call "inner speech" – when your brain hosts its own debate club in your head – rehashing past conversations, rehearsing future ones, or analyzing decisions you've made. While this internal dialogue can be valuable for problem-solving, it can also become a significant distraction

---

2. Mind-wandering is a broader term. It refers to any thoughts that are unrelated to the task at hand or the immediate environment. This can happen during any activity and often occurs without us realizing it. For example, thinking about what to have for dinner while you're in a meeting is mind-wandering.

3. Daydreaming is a specific type of mind-wandering. It typically involves more elaborate and fantastical thoughts or scenarios. Daydreams are often more immersive and story-like. In essence, all daydreaming is a form of mind-wandering, but not all mind-wandering is daydreaming. Mind-wandering can be brief and mundane, while daydreaming tends to be more vivid and extended.

when left unchecked – it can turn your head into a noisy meeting room where everyone's talking at once, and they're all you!

"Anything But This" Syndrome

We've all been there – having an irresistible feeling to reorganize your entire desk right before a crucial deadline. This "urge to diverge" is your brain's clever way of avoiding or procrastinating challenging work – like when you suddenly remember you need to color-code all your files the night before a big presentation.

Earworm Invasion

Earworms – those stubborn songs that loop in your head – are more than just annoying. I know this all too well; I once struggled to get "Another Day of Sun" out of my head while racing to meet a submission deadline for my PhD thesis. Studies show 90% of people experience them, with 15% finding them seriously disruptive to their concentration. There's nothing quite like trying to finish an important task while your brain insists on playing "Who Let the Dogs Out?" on repeat - it's just your brain's way of adding an unwanted soundtrack to your day.

Body Demands

Finally, there's your body's basic needs – hunger, fatigue, stress, or that urgent bathroom break. These aren't minor annoyances; they're your body's way of demanding attention. Research shows that basic physical needs, particularly hunger, can significantly impair decision-making and cognitive function - it's hard to focus on spreadsheets when your stomach is growling loudly craving something to eat. These aren't just inconveniences – they're legitimate barriers to maintaining focus.

The External Distraction Minefield

While internal distractions bubble up from our minds, external distractions come from our environment. From notification pings and office chatter to incoming emails, these external interruptions can derail even our best-laid plans.

Life Getting Loud

Our ears are constantly under siege in the modern workplace. From the gentle hum of the office printer to full-blown construction noise outside your window, auditory distractions are everywhere. And it's not just about volume – research shows that unexpected or irregular sounds are particularly disruptive to our concentration, and significantly decrease performance on cognitive tasks. Even a quiet office can become a symphony of small sounds: keyboard clicks, coffee maker gurgles, and whispered conversations that your brain can't help but tune into.

The Visual Vortex

Our eyes can betray our focus just as easily as our ears. Visual distractions come in all forms – a flickering fluorescent light, movement outside your window, or even just the constant parade of people walking past your desk. Research shows these visual interruptions do more than just catch our eye – they measurably increase the time it takes to complete tasks, especially when we're doing focus-intensive work. Even something as simple as a cluttered desk can become a visual distraction as your eyes (and then your thoughts) wander to each item.

Digital Disruptions

In our hyper-connected world, digital distractions have become particularly challenging to manage. Studies report we receive an average of 63.5 phone notifications daily, mostly from messaging apps. But it gets more interesting – we typically check our phones about 58 times per day, with 30 of those checks happening during work hours. Each peek lasts about 1 minute and 15 seconds, adding up to 37.5 minutes of lost work time daily.

The real kicker? We spend roughly 2.5 hours of each workday on websites and content unrelated to our jobs. Most of these digital detours are brief – less than 2 minutes – but they occur every few minutes. This constant switching between tasks can waste up to 40% of our productive time. It's not just about the time spent looking at our screens; it's about the mental energy required to repeatedly refocus on what we were doing before getting distracted - no wonder our to-do lists keep growing!

The Human Factor

Then there's the most complex distraction of all – other people! Face-to-face interruptions have a unique power to mess with our focus. Whether it's a colleague who "just needs a minute" (that turns into twenty) or an impromptu meeting that hijacks your afternoon, human interruptions are particularly challenging because they often require immediate attention and social engagement.

Research shows these in-person interruptions are among the most disruptive forms of distraction, significantly increasing the likelihood of errors in our work. Why? Because they not only break our concentration but also often require us to switch mental gears entirely – from focused individual work to social interaction and back again. Just like trying to read a book: every time you look up, you need to find your place again, remember what you just read, and get back into the flow of the story.

True Impact of Distraction

We often dismiss distractions as minor annoyances, but science tells a different story. Research reveals that these interruptions exact a hefty toll – depleting corporate profits, degrading our work quality, and disrupting our mental processes in ways that might surprise you. Let's examine the real price we pay for our fragmented attention.

Economic Impact

The numbers paint a stark picture. A survey of 1,600 people revealed that 60% rarely achieve even an hour of uninterrupted focus-intensive work daily. Even more concerning, nearly one-third can maintain focus for only 10 minutes or less before getting distracted. We spend just half our workday on actual work, with the rest lost to distractions and unproductive activities.

The financial implications are staggering. A study of a major U.S. manufacturer found that 93.6% of their annual productivity loss came from employees being distracted at work. And only 6.4% was due to actual sick days. Think about that – distracted employees cost the company 15 times more than those who called in sick[4] . On a national scale, U.S. knowledge workers lose an average of 2.1 hours daily to unimportant distractions and refocusing time – that's 25% of a typical workday! The annual cost? An estimated $588 billion, exceeding the combined GDP of Portugal and Greece.

This productivity crisis isn't limited to the US. German research shows that employees in knowledge-intensive jobs face interruptions every four minutes – about 15 times per hour. These disruptions cost German companies an estimated 114 billion euros annually, with workers losing three full days each month to distraction.

Why are these costs so high? Because each interruption creates a cascade effect. It's not just about the time directly lost – you need additional time to refocus and often must correct mistakes made while

4. This pattern has been consistently observed across different countries. A similar study in Poland confirmed these findings, suggesting this is a global phenomenon. This suggests that companies might better improve productivity by addressing workplace distractions rather than focusing solely on improving health programs for their employees.

not fully concentrating. The message is clear: distractions aren't minor inconveniences but a severe drain on productivity, affecting companies and economies on a scale that's difficult to comprehend.

Work Quality Impact

Distractions do more than just slow us down – they fundamentally alter the quality of our work in several critical ways:

Error Rates: Research reveals a direct link between interruptions and mistakes. Studies show that disruptions can double the error rate in simple tasks, with longer interruptions leading to even higher rates. In high-stakes environments, the consequences are particularly concerning – healthcare studies found that each interruption increases clinical errors by 12.7%[5] .

Consistency Problems: When constantly interrupted, we struggle to maintain a coherent approach to our work. Research shows that the start-stop-restart cycle of interrupted work makes it difficult to keep consistent standards. A report might begin with one style or approach but, after multiple interruptions, end with something completely different.

Lost Details: To compensate for lost time, we often rush through tasks after interruptions. Studies show this acceleration comes at a cost – we pay less attention to details and miss important elements of our work. Additionally, work completed in distraction-heavy environments typically requires more revisions later, ultimately taking more time than if done with full attention initially.

The implications are clear: while we might eventually complete our tasks despite interruptions, the quality of our work suffers significantly. What starts as a small distraction can cascade into substantial quality issues, requiring additional time for corrections and revisions.

---

5. These findings highlight how distractions can impact work quality across different fields, from routine tasks to critical professional work where accuracy is essential.

Cognitive Impact

Our brain's response to distractions explains why they are so draining. It's a process that unfolds in several stages:

It often begins when you're in a flow state - that perfect zone where work feels effortless and time flies by. Then a distraction hits, and your brain must perform a complete mental gear shift. This isn't just pressing pause - it's more like having to close one program to open another, requiring significant mental resources.

What makes this particularly challenging is what happens next. Even after dealing with the interruption, your brain experiences what scientists call "*attention residue*[6]." It's a kind of a "mental hangover" where part of your mind continues to process the interruption even when you think you've moved on. It's like trying to write a report while a conversation from earlier keeps playing in your head. This residual attention makes it harder to fully engage with your original task.

The cycle, then, gets pricey as the day progresses. Each interruption triggers a tiny release of stress hormones and requires additional mental energy to refocus. Your brain's ability to form clear memories also suffers, as interrupted work creates gaps in how information is processed and stored. By day's end, all these small cognitive hits add up to significant mental fatigue.

The key insight here is that your brain has a limited daily allowance of mental energy for focused work. Each distraction depletes this budget, leading to reduced productivity, increased stress, and impaired memory formation. This explains why a day filled with interruptions can leave you feeling mentally exhausted, even if you haven't completed much actual work.

---

6. The continued cognitive processing of a previous task that impairs current performance, even after switching focus to the original task.

Career Impact

Distractions don't just affect our daily work – they can significantly shape our long-term career trajectory. Research reveals three key areas where chronic interruptions take their toll:

Motivation and Energy: Constant interruptions create a cycle of "starting-stopping-restarting" that gradually depletes motivation. Studies show this pattern frequently leads to mental fatigue and burnout. The continuous drain on mental resources makes it increasingly difficult to maintain enthusiasm and energy for challenging work.

Job Satisfaction: Imagine every time you get closer to solving a puzzle someone scatters the pieces – that's how chronic interruptions prevent task completion and affect job satisfaction. Research indicates that the inability to see projects through to completion due to constant disruptions significantly decreases work fulfillment. This frustration builds up over time as achievements remain elusive.

Career Progression: The long-term consequences can be serious. Chronic dissatisfaction often leads to higher turnover rates as employees seek less disruptive work environments. More critically, the cumulative effect of interrupted work – reduced quality, increased stress, and diminished accomplishment – can obstruct career advancement opportunities.

All these effects compound over time. While an occasional distracted day might not seem like a big deal, months or years of chronic interruptions can fundamentally derail your career –getting you miles off course, wondering if you'll ever be able to reach your destination!

Putting It All Together

Throughout this chapter, we've uncovered the true scope and impact of workplace distractions. What emerges is a clear picture: distractions are far more costly than they appear on the surface, and their impact varies significantly based on our work type. Focus-intensive tasks, requiring deep concentration, are particularly vulnerable, while light-processing work offers some natural resistance – though no type of work is completely immune.

We face a dual challenge: internal distractions emerging from our own minds and bodies, and external ones assaulting us from our environment. Both types demand our attention and disrupt our focus in different but equally significant ways. Their impact cascades through multiple levels:

- Economically, costing businesses billions in lost productivity.
- Degrading work quality through errors and inconsistencies.
- Draining cognitive resources and creating lasting "attention residue."
- Gradually eroding motivation, job satisfaction, and career growth.

Perhaps most importantly, we've seen that the real cost of distractions isn't just in the moment they occur. Like compound interest working in reverse, each interruption creates effects that ripple outward, affecting not just our current task but our entire workday – and ultimately, our career trajectory.

Understanding these impacts is crucial for developing effective strategies to protect our attention. Remember: managing distractions isn't just about getting more done – it's about preserving mental energy, reducing stress, and creating space for our best work.

7

Habit Hurdles

"We first make our habits, and then our habits make us."
-John Dryden

Mind on Autopilot

Your brain makes about 35,000 decisions each day, but you're only consciously aware of a tiny fraction of them. The rest operate on autopilot – controlled by habits we've built over time. Every time you reach for your phone upon waking or snack mindlessly during TV time, you're experiencing this automation in action.

These automatic behaviors are mental shortcuts that form through repetition. In his book "The Power of Habit," Charles Duhigg explains this process through what he calls the "habit loop": it begins with a "cue" - the trigger that initiates the behavior, followed by the "behavior" itself - the automatic response, and ends with a "reward" - the payoff that reinforces the pattern.

This reinforcement mechanism is more than just repetition—it's a sophisticated adaptation that happens in your brain. Each repeated behavior is like clearing and smoothing a trail through a dense forest – that's a mental pathway under construction. The first time you perform an action, it requires significant mental effort. With each repetition, the path becomes wider, clearer, and easier to traverse.

Initially, a behavior might feel challenging or require conscious thought. Over time, your brain optimizes this pathway, reducing the mental energy required. The first few times you check your phone in the morning, it takes deliberate effort. Eventually, your hand reaches for the device almost before you're fully awake—a testament to the brain's remarkable efficiency in automating reinforced behaviors.

The habit formation process is governed by your autopilot system in the basal ganglia[1] . However, the brain doesn't distinguish between beneficial and harmful habits—it simply seeks to make frequently repeated behaviors more effortless – using less mental energy. A habit of morning meditation can become as automatic as a habit of mindless scrolling. The key difference lies in **the choices you make and consistently reinforce**.

In this chapter, we'll examine how these automatic behaviors profoundly impact our ability to focus and discover how understanding our habits might be the key to regaining manual control of our concentration.

Habit-Focus Connection

Your habits and focus share a symbiotic relationship - each constantly influencing and shaping the other. Just as habits can strengthen or weaken

---

1. The basal ganglia are a group of brain structures involved in habit formation, movement control, learning, and decision-making. They work as your brain's automation center, helping convert repeated behaviors into effortless routines.

your ability to concentrate, your focus can reinforce or break these behavioral patterns[2]. Understanding this two-way interaction is crucial for developing better concentration and more effective routines.

The Upside

Good habits can significantly enhance your concentration abilities, much like regular exercise strengthens a muscle. Consider the practice of setting aside dedicated time for focus-intensive work. By eliminating distractions and creating a consistent environment for deep concentration, you're training your brain to maintain sustained attention.

Research reports that people who regularly engage in focused, single-task work don't just get more done – they're actually rewiring their brains. Brain imaging studies reveal that sustained attention periods not only activate networks associated with cognitive control and working memory but strengthen these neural pathways over time. Those who practice this habit consistently outperform multitaskers on cognitive tasks. Simply put, the more you practice focused work sessions, the better your brain becomes at maintaining attention and resisting distractions.[3]

The Dark side

Conversely, some habits can seriously impair your focus. Something like the common habit of checking your phone first thing in the morning. This is when you've just opened your eyes, and before your feet even hit

---

2. A symbiotic relationship is a partnership where both sides affect each other, like when you have a friend who loves to cook, and you love to eat. When you hang out, they get to practice their cooking (which makes them happy), and you get delicious food (which makes you happy), and both benefit from the interaction. This back-and-forth influence can be either beneficial or harmful, depending on the situation.

3. Building on our earlier discussion of brain plasticity in chapter 2, studies show that consistent focus training leads to measurable changes in brain activity, improving working memory and attention control.

the floor, your hand is already reaching for your smartphone. Sounds familiar, right? This supposedly innocent habit might feel as natural as stretching, but it's actually setting the tone for a day full of distraction. You're essentially inviting the entire world into your brain before even having the chance to set your priorities for the day.

So, how many times you check your phone in the first hour of waking up? Research reveals that frequent phone checking is linked to increased "cognitive failures" – forgotten appointments, less productivity, and even accidents from divided attention. But the consequences go beyond that - what's happening in your brain is particularly concerning[4] . Your brain naturally maintains a healthy baseline of dopamine (your reward chemical), but frequent social media use gradually depletes this reserve and dulls your reward sensors. Like building a tolerance to a drug, you begin needing more stimulation to feel the same satisfaction. This creates a vicious cycle: more scrolling for diminishing returns, which leaves your dopamine tank empty, leading to what's now known as "brain rot[5] ."

Over the long-term, this pattern of high dopamine consumption and low production doesn't just fragment your attention – it can lead to decreased motivation, chronic anxiety, and depression[6] . Through this seemingly harmless habitual behavior, your brain's reward system essentially becomes rewired, making it harder to find satisfaction in normal activities while craving the quick hits of social media stimulation.

---

4. Recent studies link specific digital behaviors to neurochemical changes, affecting dopamine baseline levels and receptor sensitivity. A three-year study demonstrated how checking habits reshape the brain's reward circuitry over time.

5. Brain rot, Oxford's 2024 word of the year, refers to mental deterioration caused by overconsumption of trivial online content. Social media addicts often report severe lack of energy and motivation, struggling to leave their beds or couches—a direct result of dopamine depletion from nonstop scrolling.

6. Research indicates that while social media can temporarily boost mood through social validation, excessive use often leads to decreased satisfaction, increased anxiety, and mood disorders.

Tending Your Habit Garden

Now that we understand how habits and focus interact, let's look into your "habit garden" – the behavioral patterns you've cultivated over time. Some are deliberately planted, others have grown wild, but all affect your ability to focus.

Take a moment to imagine your mind as a vast garden where habits grow like seeds you plant daily. Each time you repeat a behavior, you're watering these seeds, helping them grow stronger. Your habit garden is constantly evolving. Like a time-lapse video, your daily habits grow and spread over weeks, months, and years. Today's small habit could become tomorrow's mighty oak of concentration, or if neglected, might overrun your entire mental landscape. For that, we need to weigh up the seeds you have in your habit garden to examine how different habits can either nourish or deplete your focus.

Nurturing Growth

Regular physical exercise is one of the best habits you need to cultivate. Like any good habit, exercise's benefits compound over time. Working out regularly develops your brain's capacity for concentration and cognitive agility. Studies consistently demonstrate that it does much more than building your muscle – it enhances memory, sharpens attention, and boosts problem-solving skills. The endorphins released during exercise also reduce stress and improve mood, creating optimal conditions for sustained focus[7]. This makes physical activity a beneficial seed to grow for both your mental and physical fitness. So, next time you're debating whether to hit the gym or hit the couch, you already know the answer!

---

7. Endorphins produced during exercise create a "runner's high" – this brief state of relaxation and euphoria you reach during physical exercise. It's kind of a happiness cocktail that makes you feel-good and chilled out. Another reason to be into working out, right?

Deceptive Blooms

Our garden inventory reveals some attractive but dangerous growth patterns – habits that masquerade as productivity boosters while secretly sap your focus.

Procrastination: Putting things off forms like any other habit: you face a challenging task (trigger), delay it for something else (response behavior), and feel temporary relief (reward). This cycle reinforces itself, and procrastination becomes your go-to response. What makes this habit alluring is the illusion of being productive – after all, you're still doing something, just not the priority task. Research shows that this behavior often stems from self-handicapping[8] , with the immediate dopamine reward making the habit particularly sticky.

While procrastination might provide short-term comfort, studies reveal that procrastinators not only produce lower quality work but also face increased stress when finally tackling delayed tasks. More concerning is what psychologists call "*goal deactivation*" – repeated delays gradually disconnect your brain from its objectives, making future focus on them even harder.

Multitasking: Another deceptive habit is multitasking – a seed many pursue believing it could grow multiple fruits at once, but in reality, it produces lower quality ones while exhausting your garden.

What we call multitasking is actually rapid task-switching, and research shows it's remarkably inefficient. Each switch depletes mental energy and

8. Self-handicapping is a psychological defense mechanism where people avoid tasks by deliberately creating obstacles (like delaying work until the last minute) to have a ready excuse for potential failure, and like this protect their self-esteem. For example, when someone says, "I could have done better if I'd started earlier," they're using procrastination as a self-handicapping strategy to create a safety net attributing any shortcomings to lack of time rather than ability. While this temporarily protects self-image, it creates a cycle of avoidance that ultimately undermines both performance and personal growth.

increases stress, while the small dopamine treats we get every time we jump between tasks reinforce this counterproductive pattern. The behavior itself emerges from workload pressures, but it also can surface as a result of FOMO (fear of missing out). A study found that people who frequently check their devices for fear of missing out important information or social opportunities are the most likely to engage in task-switching.

Ironically, those who consider themselves excellent multitaskers typically perform worst at it[9]. This overconfidence leads to poor choices. Students, for instance, often believe they can effectively study while watching TV or browsing social media, yet research shows this significantly reduces both task completion time and full comprehension. The cognitive cost is substantial: every task switch requires your brain to refocus when you return back to it, creating accumulating delays and mental fatigue.

When the spotlight of your attention is focused on one task, it brightly shines every detail, yet when the beam is split between multiple tasks, each area receives weaker illumination. Studies reveal that habitual multitaskers struggle more with focusing on relevant information and ignoring distractions[10]. Even more striking, brain imaging shows that "*heavy media multitaskers*[11]" have less gray matter - the brain's processor, remember? - in regions crucial for attention control. This suggests that the habit of multitasking might literally be reshaping our brains – and not for the better.

---

9. A classic example of the Dunning-Kruger effect – a cognitive bias where people with limited skills in an area overestimate their abilities.

10. Research shows that frequent multitasking not only impairs productivity but also increases error rates and compromises cognitive performance, particularly when dealing with demanding tasks.

11. Heavy media multitaskers -those who frequently engage with multiple forms of digital media simultaneously – for example, browsing social media while watching videos, texting while reading online articles, or juggling multiple communication platforms at once. Researchers typically identify them by their pattern of regularly consuming multiple streams of digital content rather than focusing on one media source at a time.

Invasive Species

Just as a garden can become overrun with weeds, your mental clarity can be attacked by some harmful growths threatening your ability to focus.

Physical Clutter: A disorganized physical environment does more than make it hard to find your important stuff – it actively drains your attention. Like creeping vines, clutter gradually spreads its influence, with each item nibbling away at your cognitive resources. The habit of maintaining a messy space makes it increasingly difficult for your brain to maintain focus.

Digital Overwhelm: Your digital environment requires equal attention. Like a greenhouse left permanently open to every passing breeze, the habit of staying constantly connected doesn't just fragment your attention – it creates a mental fog through infinite information overload. Our minds, once cultivated for deep engagement through reading and sustained thought, have gradually adapted to shallow, rapid-fire digital consumption. Just as a garden's soil can change with different farming practices, our brains have rewired themselves for quick, disposable information rather than deep processing. As notifications endlessly flood in, distinguishing important signals from noise becomes increasingly difficult, leaving you tending to distractions rather than nurturing what matters. Studies show that heavy digital media users develop shorter attention spans and decreased productivity, as their cognitive resources get consumed by managing digital chaos rather than focusing on meaningful work. Those who set boundaries and create dedicated offline time, however, maintain better focus and productivity – showing that just as our minds adapted to digital chaos, they can be recultivated for deeper focus.

Garden Killers

Think you've seen the worst already? Wait until you meet the most destructive habits in your mental garden – the equivalent of cultivating kudzu vines[12] ! These don't just compete with healthy growth but completely choke it out. Consider those late-night Netflix binges coupled with midnight snacking – hosting a nightly party when your brain needs quiet time to reset and prepare for tomorrow.

Studies indicate that irregular eating patterns, especially late-night refrigerator raids, do more than add extra calories – they throw off your entire biological clock. When you stay up late binging shows and snacking, you're preventing your brain from performing its crucial nighttime maintenance. The result is a double whammy: disrupted sleep patterns and compromised cognitive function the next day.

This chaos doesn't stay contained. Like kudzu smothering everything in its path, these nighttime habits gradually overrun your mental landscape, affecting everything from memory and attention to decision-making ability. Once established, these patterns become particularly difficult to change, making them among the most dangerous habits in your mental garden.

Putting It All Together

The relationship between habits and focus mirrors the delicate balance of a thriving garden. Our analysis to this connection demonstrated how automated behaviors – from morning routines to late-night habits – shape our cognitive landscape.

In our habit garden inventory, we looked at four distinct types of growth patterns that affect our mental clarity:

- Practicing exercise and focused work strengthens cognitive pathways.

12. Kudzu, nicknamed "the vine that ate the South," is an aggressive plant that grows at lightning speed, blocking sunlight and smothering everything in its path - trees, buildings, you name it. It's an apt metaphor for habits that quickly take over and smother healthy mental patterns.

- Engaging in procrastination and multitasking creates an illusion of productivity.
- Allowing physical clutter and digital overwhelm gradually depletes attention.
- Maintaining poor night-time routines disrupts our brain's essential maintenance.

The key insight? Just as a garden requires intentional tending, our habits need conscious cultivation. Understanding the symbiotic relationship between habits and focus is the first step. The next is recognizing that every repeated behavior is like watering a seed – we're either nurturing concentration or feeding distractions. In essence, a weed is just a plant in the wrong place – it's up to you to decide what grows and what goes.

As we move forward, remember that changing habits isn't about uprooting everything at once. It's about gradually cultivating patterns that support focused work while mindfully managing those that undermine it. At the end of the day, your mental garden will always keep growing – the question is, what are you choosing to water in it?

8

Energy Drain

"It's nature's way of telling you something's wrong."
-Spirit

The Many Faces of Fatigue

Three hours into your workday, and your brain's already waving a white flag. It's barely midday, and your morning clarity has vanished, replaced by a mental haze that makes reading a report feel like decoding hieroglyphics. At that point, your mind just hit the snooze button – again. Ring a bell?

But this isn't just about being tired – it's far more nuanced. Our energy reserves aren't just a simple gas tank that goes from full to empty. They're more like a complex power grid, where different systems can fail in unique ways. Learning about the different types of energy drain is indispensable if you're after maintaining a sharp focus throughout the day.

Physical Exhaustion

Anyone who's pulled an all-nighter or spent a day moving furniture knows physical fatigue intimately – when your legs feel like lead and your eyelids seem weighted. But this isn't just your body asking for rest; research shows it's a critical alarm system for your brain to recharge.

Studies reveal that sleep deprivation acts like kryptonite for cognitive performance - particularly attention and working memory. More surprisingly, lack of sleep impacts your mood even more severely than it affects thinking or movement. When you ignore your body's need for rest, both focus and emotional balance become the first casualties.

Mental Drain

Even after a good night's sleep, intense cognitive work can leave your brain feeling scrambled. Whether you've spent hours on a complex project, crammed for an exam, or handled a personal crisis, simple cognitive tasks become challenging – as if you're wading through molasses.

What's fascinating is that mental fatigue isn't confined to your brain. When your mind is exhausted, your entire body gets the shutdown signal. Try hitting the gym after an intellectually-demanding day, and you might struggle with weights that usually feel light or find yourself winded during a typically easy run. It's not laziness – it's your brain and body's coordinated response to cognitive overload.

Lifestyle-Induced Fatigue

That persistent exhaustion might have a simpler explanation than you think: your daily choices. When your routine consists of late-night streaming, drive-thru dinners, and minimal physical activity, you become the architect of your own energy crisis.

Research shows that poor lifestyle habits create a compound effect on fatigue. Diets high in processed foods and sugars trigger a roller coaster of energy spikes and crashes. Studies report that consuming fast food more than twice weekly significantly increases chronic fatigue. Surprisingly, while sedentary behavior depletes energy, regular exercise – even when you're tired – actually boosts energy levels.[1]

Think of your body as a finely-tuned machine: like a car, it needs quality fuel and regular maintenance. Feed it junk and let it rust on the couch, and it'll run like junk. The good news? These lifestyle factors are within your control, making this form of fatigue particularly actionable.

Medical Fatigue

Sometimes exhaustion persists despite healthy eating, adequate sleep, and regular exercise. When you're constantly running on low power mode regardless of rest, it might signal that your body's energy management system needs medical attention.

Like a phone with a damaged battery – no amount of charging gets it past 20%. This is the reality for people with certain health conditions that affect energy levels. Conditions like anemia[2], thyroid disorders[3], and Chronic Fatigue Syndrome[4] can drain energy reserves faster than they can

---

1. Research demonstrates that diet quality directly impacts energy levels, sleep quality, and next-day alertness. Regular physical activity, despite initial fatigue, helps boost overall energy levels.

2. Anemia occurs when blood can't effectively carry oxygen, resulting in persistent fatigue.

3. Thyroid is the body's thermostat and energy regulator. Therefore, thyroid disorders disrupt the body's energy regulation system, affecting overall energy levels.

4. Chronic Fatigue Syndrome (CFS) causes extreme exhaustion that doesn't improve with rest, making even simple daily activities challenging.

be replenished. Unlike normal tiredness that improves with rest, this type of fatigue is persistent and significantly impacts quality of life.

If you find yourself constantly exhausted despite good habits, consider consulting a healthcare provider. Sometimes fatigue isn't just about needing more sleep – it might be your body signaling an underlying issue that requires attention.

Fatigue Fallout

Picture your well-rested brain as a sophisticated system processing information, filtering out distractions and maintaining attention with precision. But when fatigue sets in, this delicate machinery begins to malfunction in several critical ways:

Cognitive Slowdown: Fatigue unplugs a bunch of important cables making your sharp mind turns sluggish. Your processing speed drops impairing your ability to concentrate and think clearly. It's like trying to run complex software on a computer with a dying battery.

Compromised Filtering: Research shows that fatigue significantly impairs your brain's ability to filter information. Your usually effective distraction barrier becomes porous, letting in irrelevant stimuli that would normally be blocked. Even more concerning, studies reveal that fatigue alters how you perceive information, making you miss important cues while misinterpreting others.

Fatigue-Stress Loop: Perhaps most insidious is how fatigue creates a self-reinforcing cycle with stress. When fatigue hits, work take longer to complete - tasks you usually finish in an hour will stretch into two or three. As a result, work will pile up amplifying your worries. This stress then interferes with sleep quality, leading to more fatigue the next day, which will make you more stressed for being less productive. Research shows that chronic fatigue actually heightens your brain's response to stress, making you more sensitive to negative emotional stimuli. Each element – fatigue, and stress, feeds into the others, creating a challenging cycle to break.

Putting It All Together

Fatigue manifests in multiple forms, each uniquely capable of derailing your focus. Like a sophisticated power grid, different systems can fail in distinct ways – from physical exhaustion and mental drain to lifestyle-induced and medical fatigue. When these energy systems falter, they trigger a cascade of effects that compromise your ability to concentrate.

The key to winning isn't pushing through when exhausted - it's about honoring your body's signals and responding appropriately. Mental clarity starts with respecting the right of your mind in rest and recovery. After all, **a well-rested mind is a focused mind**.

9

Stress Spiral

"Stress is like spice. Too little produces a bland, dull meal; too much may choke you." -Donald Tubesing

Inner Storm

Your brain runs like a high-end computer, with cognitive functions operating like perfectly synced programs. But when stress creeps in, your processor starts choking, and your mental battery drains faster than you can imagine – transforming crystal-clear thinking into mental static.

Stress triggers a flood of chemicals in your body – starting an inner storm which activates your body's emergency response system. That's useful when facing genuine threats, less helpful when you're just facing deadlines! It's like your brain's alarm system misfiring, preparing for survival when you only need to survive a submission due date.

Anxiety follows in stress's wake, transforming immediate concerns into a constant hum of anticipated troubles. If stress is the storm, anxiety is the forecast that never stops predicting rain– that constant background process running "what-if" scenarios. While stress responds to immediate pressures, anxiety anticipates future ones.

Together, they create a powerful duo that splits your attention between present demands and imagined future worries, making it incredibly challenging to focus on anything and be productive. Therefore, in this chapter, we'll try to understand how they deplete our mental energy and tamper with our concentration - a crucial first step toward maintaining focus in our high-pressure world.

Origins of Stress

Workplace Pressure: Modern workplaces often operate like pressure cookers set permanently to "high." With endless deadlines and exponentially growing to-do lists, stress becomes a constant companion. Studies report an increasingly concerning picture across industries and cultures – while 44% of Americans report feeling stressed during their workday, global surveys reveal an even more alarming reality, with 84% of workers experiencing regular stress exposure.

The primary culprits? Overwhelming workload tops the list, followed closely by office politics – from conflict to micromanagement. Perhaps the most infamous reason the survey respondents mentioned was the "always-on" culture, where the necessity to be 24/7 available blurs the line between work and rest. No wonder our minds often dwell on workplace disputes instead of focusing on actual work!

Life Uncertainties: You might think that once you clock out, you're in the clear. But stress and anxiety aren't exactly respectful of work-life boundaries, so they follow you home. For example:

- Financial worries gnaw at your concentration like a persistent toothache.
- Relationship challenges demand mental energy.
- Health concerns (yours or loved ones') create background anxiety.
- Modern pressures like social media comparison and the fear of missing out (FOMO) breed frustration and contribute to personal stress, draining your mental energy[1] .

These work and life pressures don't exist in isolation – they mix and merge like ingredients in a personalized stress soup. In other words, everyone's stress recipe is unique. What causes overwhelming anxiety in one might barely register with another, making it crucial to identify your personal stress triggers. After all, you can't defuse a bomb without first mapping its wires.

Price of Pressure

Mental Impact: Stress and anxiety aren't just feelings – they trigger a cascade of biological changes. When these states become chronic, stress hormones like cortisol and adrenaline start playing a twisted game of "brain Jenga"- pulling out crucial pieces and hoping the whole tower doesn't fall down. Research shows that chronic stress induces brain rewiring (i.e. physical alteration of brain structure), particularly in regions

1. The constant parade of achievements and highlights on social media invites endless self-comparison. Research shows that limiting social media use to 30 minutes per day significantly reduced loneliness, depression, and FOMO while improving concentration. This social comparison creates 'attention residue'—emotional effects that continue to occupy mental bandwidth even after logging off.

controlling attention and brain management functions. It's as if stress is renovating your mind, but this remodeling progressively downgrades your brain's operating system - leaving you with a glitchy version.

Anxiety creates its own form of cognitive chaos. Something reminiscent of attentional tug-of-war: your task on one end, worried thoughts on the other, with your mental resources stretched thin between them. Like trying to watch two shows simultaneously, you catch pieces of both but fully engage with neither.

Physical Impact: Stress and anxiety manifest physically turning your body into their playground. They trigger headaches, muscle tension, stomach butterflies, and persistent fatigue. These physical symptoms aren't just discomfort – research shows they significantly impact cognitive function. Each physical manifestation acts like a persistent tap on your shoulder, continuously pulling attention away from your tasks.

Perhaps most damaging is the stress-fatigue spiral we explored earlier. Stress disrupts sleep, leading to increased fatigue, which elevates stress sensitivity. As productivity suffers, worries amplify, and the cycle of discomfort and distraction continues. What starts as pressure in the mind reverberates through your entire body, creating a system-wide performance lag, affecting everything from decision-making to concentration.

Putting It All Together

Understanding how pressure affects your focus is like gathering valuable intel. By spotting the roots of stress in your life – from workplace demands to personal uncertainties – you've taken the first step toward managing their impact, which we'll explore in detail in the next part of this book.

There's an important silver lining in this knowledge: research shows that simply reframing how we view stress can improve our performance under pressure. Instead of seeing it as a pure threat, try viewing it as your body's way of rising to a challenge – an opportunity for growth rather than a barrier.

Above all, stress and anxiety are universal human experiences that affect everyone, from CEOs to baristas. Once understood, they can be better managed. Let this knowledge be your foundation for maintaining focus in the face of any pressure.

10

Emotion Shift

"Emotions are the colors of the soul." -William P. Young

Emotional Palette

Picture your mind as a living canvas, where emotions paint your experiences in vibrant hues. Some days bring sky blue of calmness, others splash fierce reds of frustration, and occasionally, everything gets washed in the gray mist of uncertainty. Your emotional palette doesn't just affect your mood – it profoundly impacts your ability to concentrate, and this is what we will analyze in this chapter.

Understanding the Colors

To navigate our mental landscape effectively, we need to distinguish between three distinct aspects of our emotional experience. While many people group emotions, feelings, and moods into one general category of "how we feel," each plays a unique role in coloring our experiences – like different elements of an artist's palette.

Emotions are like pure, unmixed colors – intense and brief responses to specific events. They're the bright yellow streak of joy when you ace an exam or the sharp red flash of anger when stuck in traffic. These are your primary colors - bold and unmistakable.

Feelings emerge when emotions blend with thoughts and interpretations. Like mixing that pure yellow of joy with your thoughts of all what you've been through to ace the exam, and this will create a warm orange of pride. They're your conscious experience of emotions, refined by context and personal meaning.

Moods act as your canvas' background tones, persisting longer and coloring everything you experience. A blue mood of sadness tints your entire perspective and how you see everything else on the canvas, while a mood of fulfillment might fill your canvas with a soft, warm glow that adds a pleasant tone to every experience.

The living canvas of our mind is continuously changing by these interacting aspects of our emotional palette. Throughout the day, our experiences typically divide into two main emotional collections, each uniquely affecting our ability to focus:

Bright Collection

Positive emotions like joy, interest, and excitement fill your mental canvas with vibrant yellows and oranges – creating cheerful collection. Research shows these emotions typically enhance problem-solving and creativity.

However, this expanded perspective can sometimes distract you more. Excitement, for instance, might scatter your attention through hopping from one task to another, making it harder to complete any single one.

Dark Collection

Darker emotions like sadness, anxiety, and anger tend to constrict your mental canvas that it feels smaller. When experiencing these emotions, you might find yourself trapped in tunnel vision – either fixating on minute details while missing the bigger picture, or feeling so unstable in your focus that you make more mistakes, work with a slower pace, or procrastinate altogether.

Emotional Masterpieces

Now that we've surveyed our emotional collections, let's examine some key masterpieces that are there in the gallery and play crucial roles in shaping our ability to focus in ways that deserve special attention.

Anxiety – Misty Portrait

Building on our earlier discussion of how anxiety is the lingering aftermath of stress. Anxiety is the persistent mist hovering over your mental landscape and making everything appear less defined. But this isn't just simple blur – anxiety actively exaggerates the shadows, making them loom larger and appear more threatening. Research shows that anxiety crowds your mental space with an endless stream of "what-if" scenarios and sketches of things that might go wrong. Your usually sharp, and clear mental picture remains recognizable but requires significantly more effort to bring into focus – like trying to discern details through a fog that never quite lifts. Eventually, this divides your attention between focusing on your tasks and fighting with potential worries.

Sadness – Dark Blues

Deep, somber blues dominate this emotional portrait, where everything appears to be drawn toward a central point. Like a black hole in the canvas, sadness pulls your attention away from the external world and into your inner thoughts. Whether triggered by loss, disappointment, or unmet expectations, even subtle touches of this blue tint can dramatically alter how you process information and maintain focus.

Let me share a personal experience that illustrates this emotion's power. Years ago, while finishing my PhD abroad, my father passed away on New Year's Eve. Unable to fly home, I went to the lab, seeking distraction through work. Though fireworks painted the night sky with festive colors, my mental landscape remained stubbornly blue. A simple task that normally took an hour stretched into three – my sadness had consumed my focus entirely. This was not a subjective experience, as studies show sadness significantly impairs attention and memory processes, as if installing a blue filter over our mental lens that makes everything require more effort to process and retain.

Anger – Fiery Hues

Next comes anger, its portrait radiates with intense reds and oranges. Anger creates a peculiar focus effect – there's usually one element stands out while everything else fades to background blur. Like a powerful spotlight in a dark room: while brilliantly illuminating one spot, it can leave us blind to anything lurking in the shadows.

Anger works as a "push forward[1] " energy, creating a powerful forward momentum. In other words, anger makes you want to charge ahead and deal with what's bugging you. While this energy can sometimes be

---

1. Sometimes called "approach-related" emotion, meaning it often motivates us to confront or engage with the source of our anger, unlike other negative emotions that might trigger avoidance.

productive – providing courage to address injustice or confront problems – it often pushes us toward hasty action and rushed decisions. It's like running into a room without checking if the door is open first - you might bump your head!

This elevated, but narrow, focus makes anger particularly tricky for concentration. While it can supercharge attention toward specific issues, it often prevents us from seeing crucial context or considering consequences. The challenge lies in harnessing this focused energy without letting it completely override our broader awareness.

Boredom – Faded Canvas

Among our emotional portraits, there's boredom - painted in dull, washed-out colors. Unlike the bright, eye-catching pieces around it, this one blends into the background, lacking contrast and very easy to miss.

Such muted masterpiece can actually have a big impact on your ability to focus. Unlike the intense disruptions of anxiety or anger, boredom creates a different kind of attention deficit. Whether triggered by repetitive tasks or lack of challenge, boredom leaves you restless and actively pushes you to seek stimulation elsewhere, often leading to procrastination and reduced productivity.

Interestingly, researchers suggest this state might serve a valuable purpose. Rather than viewing boredom as purely negative, science indicates it could be your brain's signal to seek more engaging or meaningful activities. In this light, boredom becomes less of a barrier to focus and more of a catalyst for positive change – prompting creativity and encouraging you to pursue more stimulating challenges.

Putting It All Together

As we wrap up the tour through the emotional gallery, let's take a moment to reflect on what we've seen in it so far. Emotions, like different paintings, each have their own style and impact on your ability to focus and how we engage with tasks. There's no such thing as a "perfect" emotional artwork. Even the dark, moody pieces have their place.

The goal isn't to fill your gallery with only bright, happy paintings. Instead, it's about learning to appreciate and work with all the colors in your emotional palette. Like this, you can create a gallery that helps you concentrate better. So, you'd move a particularly intense painting to a less prominent spot if it's affecting your focus too much. Or you'd know how to channel the energy of an exciting piece into productive work.

Ultimately, mastering focus is about becoming both the artist and the curator of your emotional gallery. It's a skill you can develop, allowing your emotions to inspire and energize you without taking over the whole exhibit.

Connecting the Dots

The Focus Ecosystem

Throughout Part II, we've seen how different forces can fracture your focus, each affecting your mental ecosystem much like environmental factors influence a delicate habitat. Like the Great Barrier Reef or Amazon Rainforest, your concentration responds to countless interconnected elements.

Distractions act like rising temperatures that bleach a coral reef – each interruption spreads far beyond the moment weakening our mental resilience. Habits function as deeply rooted species in this ecosystem: some invasive, others supportive. Energy levels rise and fall like vital water supplies, while stress moves like weather patterns, capable of uprooting our carefully cultivated habits. And emotions color this landscape like changing seasons, affecting how our entire ecosystem functions.

What emerges is a crucial insight: your focus isn't just a simple spotlight that either works or doesn't. It's a complex, living system where changes in one area create ripple effects throughout – improve your sleep habits, and you'll likely find yourself more resilient to distractions, better at maintaining good routines, and more emotionally balanced. So, understanding these forces and how they interact isn't just academic – it's the foundation for developing strategies to protect and strengthen your concentration.

Mapping Your Focus Environment

Just as scientists can't protect a reef without understanding its delicate balance, we can't enhance your focus without mapping its terrain. Each person's concentration has unique patterns, challenges, and strengths. To help you understand your personal focus ecosystem, the "Distraction Diagnostic" that follows will serve as your assessment tool, measuring the health of your mental environment across all territories we've explored. It will help you identify which areas of your cognitive landscape need nurturing, protection, or restoration.

I encourage you to take this diagnostic while your understanding of your focus ecosystem is fresh. The insights you gain will guide you through the practical strategies we'll explore next.

Distraction Diagnostic

"If you can't measure it, you can't improve it."
-Lord Kelvin

Understanding Your Focus Profile

Having explored the complex nature of your focus ecosystem, it's time to measure its vital signs. "A problem well-stated is a problem half-solved," goes the saying, and that's exactly why precise assessment is crucial. Like scientists moving from general principles to specific data collection, we'll map the unique patterns of your attention landscape.

Just as measuring water quality and coral health reveals a reef's condition, understanding your focus challenges shows you the way to improvement. Each section of this diagnostic serves as a specialized tool, measuring different aspects of your cognitive environment.

This evaluation transforms understanding into action, providing clear insights into which areas of your focus ecosystem need strengthening.

Instructions: Rate each statement on a scale of 1-5:
1 = Rarely/Never.
2 = Occasionally.
3 = Sometimes.
4 = Often.
5 = Almost Always/Always.

Remember: This isn't a test to pass or fail; it's a tool for self-understanding. Your honest responses will guide your journey toward better focus.

Section A: Distraction Patterns

External Distractions:

1. I get interrupted by notifications during focus-demanding work.
2. My workspace is often noisy or full of distraction.
3. Colleagues frequently interrupt me while working.
4. Visual distractions catch my attention easily.
5. Surroundings (noise, movement, etc.) break my focus.

Digital Habits:

1. I check my phone without a specific reason.
2. I switch often between multiple tasks on my computer.
3. Social media pulls me away from important work.
4. I deal with messages immediately when they arrive.
5. Digital distractions affect my work quality.

Internal Distractions:

1. My mind wanders during important tasks.
2. I lose myself in daydreams while working.
3. Worried thoughts interrupt my concentration.
4. I find it hard to stick to one task.
5. Personal concerns distract me from work.

Section B: Habit Assessment

Focus Habits:

1. I work on multiple tasks simultaneously.
2. I check emails/messages while doing important work.
3. I skip taking breaks during long work sessions.
4. I don't follow any consistent daily routine.
5. I don't care about preparing my workspace before start working.

Environment:

1. My workspace is cluttered or disorganized.
2. I work with my phone within reach.
3. I don't have a dedicated workspace for focus-demanding tasks.
4. There are no boundaries between work and breaks.
5. I overlook my environment when I do focus-demanding work.

Routine:

1. My work patterns are irregular or unpredictable.
2. I skip meals when busy with work.
3. I don't have consistent sleep and wake times.
4. I don't plan my tasks, I just wing it.
5. I don't have specific rituals when I start focus-intensive work.

Section C: Energy Check

Physical Energy:

1. I feel physically exhausted during work.
2. I experience energy crashes during the day.
3. I can't maintain focus without caffeine.
4. I feel sleepy during important tasks.
5. Physical discomfort disrupts my concentration.

Mental Energy:

1. My mind feels foggy or unclear.
2. I struggle to process information effectively.
3. Simple decisions become tough when tired.
4. I consistently experience a significant drop in focus after meals.
5. My productivity decreases significantly late in the day.

Recovery:

1. I do not take sufficient breaks between tasks.
2. I don't get enough sleep each night.
3. I rarely engage in physical activity regularly.
4. I don't do any stress-relief-related activities.
5. I don't have strategies to manage my energy.

Section D: Stress & Anxiety Impact

Stress Indicators:

1. I feel overwhelmed by my workload.
2. I become highly stressed about deadlines.
3. I experience physical tension while working.
4. Stress significantly impacts my sleep quality.
5. I rush through tasks due to pressure.

Anxiety Patterns:

1. I worry about future tasks while working.
2. I worry a lot and it affects my concentration.
3. I am tense when I need to be focused.
4. I procrastinate because I'm afraid I won't finish what I started.
5. Mistakes make me anxious about future work.

Pressure Management:

1. I do not make time to think of stress management strategies.
2. I can't sustain focus under pressure.
3. It takes me long time to recover from stressful situations.
4. I struggle to cope with unexpected changes.
5. When stressed, I don't know how to maintain perspective.

Section E: Emotional Influence

Emotional Awareness:

1. Strong emotions disrupt my focus.
2. My mood significantly affects my work quality.
3. I struggle to recognize when emotions impact my performance.
4. I am easily frustrated when facing obstacles.
5. Emotional events affect my focus for extended periods.

Emotional Management:

1. I don't know how to work when under negative emotions.
2. I don't possess any strategies to manage emotional disruptions.
3. It's difficult to maintain professional focus during personal issues.
4. I struggle to control my emotions when facing challenging tasks.
5. It takes me long time to bounce back from emotional setbacks.

Work Impact:

1. Workplace interactions affect my emotional state.
2. Performance pressure impacts my emotional balance.
3. I don't know how to maintain my emotions during criticism.
4. Fluctuating confidence overtakes my ability to focus.
5. My emotional state interferes with effective team interactions.

Interpreting Your Results

Scoring Guide

Calculate your total score for each section (maximum 75 points per section) and overall total (maximum 375 points).

Section Scores:

15-30: Minimal impact – well managed.
31-45: Moderate impact – needs attention.
46-60: Significant impact – priority for improvement.
61-75: Severe impact – immediate intervention.

Overall Score:

75-150: Strong foundation with minimal disruption.
151-225: Moderate challenges.
226-300: Significant disruption.
301-375: Severe challenges.

Analyzing Your Profile

Your scores tell a story about your focus ecosystem. Let's break it down:

***Strength Areas* (Scores below 30)**

These well-managed areas form your focus foundation. They're your launching pad for improving other areas.

***Challenge Areas* (Scores above 46)**

These areas need priority attention. They're the pressure points in your focus ecosystem that require immediate action.

Understanding Connections

Your focus challenges often work like dominoes – when one falls, others often follow. High scores in multiple areas usually reveal important relationships:

- Stress and Energy often pair, each amplifying the other.
- Habits and Distractions frequently work together.
- Emotions can intensify any other challenge.

These connections aren't just problems – they're opportunities. Understanding how your challenges interact helps you break negative cycles and build positive ones.

This analysis provides your roadmap for the practical strategies we'll explore in Part III.

PART III

FOCUS REDEEMED

"Concentration is the secret of strength."
-Ralph Waldo Emerson

Building Your Focus Machine

Think of your focus like a high-performance vehicle waiting to be assembled. Right now, it might feel like you have all the parts scattered across your garage floor, but together, we're about to build something remarkable.

First, we'll construct your focus engine - the core powerhouse of your mental performance. We'll assemble the critical components: goal-setting systems, time management mechanisms, and habit formation techniques that will drive your concentration forward.

Next, we'll optimize everything else under the hood. Here's where it gets fascinating - just as tuning any part of a race car improves its overall performance, **enhancing your cognitive capabilities automatically upgrades your ability to focus**. Through proper nutrition, quality sleep, strategic exercise, and advanced mental resilience, we're not just maintaining the machine - we're supercharging its entire system.

Finally, we'll design the perfect track for your high-performance machine. Because even the most perfectly tuned car needs the right conditions to demonstrate its full capability. We'll create an environment, both physical and digital, that supports rather than sabotages your focus potential.

What we discuss in this part of the book will serve as an engineering guide for your focus. Not a quick tune-up, but a complete build from the ground up - creating a focus machine that's ready to perform at its absolute best.

Ready to start building?

11

Focus 101

"The bad news is time flies. The good news is you're the pilot."
-Michael Altshuler

Your Focus' Engine

Once upon a time, a student struggling with concentration went to see his mentor seeking help. "Show me your schedule," the mentor said. When presented with empty pages, the mentor smiled knowingly, and said: "How come that you want to focus when you haven't chosen a destination?"

This ancient wisdom carries a modern truth: focus requires direction. Focus is that spotlight aiming at one thing illuminating it, for that it needs a clear target. Imagine getting into your car just to 'drive somewhere' – no destination in mind. How would you know if you're making progress? Whether to turn left or right? Your mind works the same way. Without clear destinations (defined goals and structured plans), it will take any random exit, becoming an easy target for distractions. Research based on years of empirical studies reveals that our brains don't just prefer clear direction – they require it for optimal performance.

But direction alone isn't enough. Even the best-planned journey needs a proper schedule to reach its destination. That's where time enters the picture. Time is our most valuable attention currency, and unfortunately, it's non-renewable – each moment, once spent, vanishes forever. Yet many of us attempt to navigate our days without managing this precious element. As a result, our attention splits between what we are doing and anxious thinking about what to do next. It's like trying to drive while constantly rerouting your GPS – neither efficient nor safe.

Even with perfect goals and killer time management, we might still struggle to keep our spotlight steady. Why? Because we're fighting against our own ingrained habits. These automatic behaviors acting like the electrical wiring in a house – either powering our productivity or causing constant short circuits.

In this chapter, we'll construct your focus engine from the ground up. Like building a high-performance car, we won't start with the flashy paint job – we'll begin with the core components. Goals, and time management will serve as your engine's blueprint, and habits as your automatic controls. Together, these elements will form the powerful engine that drives your focus performance, keeping you steady on the road to success.

Clear Goals

Remember what we said about driving without a destination? That's your brain without clear goals. But not just any goals will do. Because having vague GPS instructions like "head somewhere north" is quite frustrating. Hence, the need of **clear goals**. That's why some studies reported that people who set specific goals showed better focus and task engagement when working than those who just "tried their best." In other words, having crystal-clear objectives make you spend way less time scrolling through cat videos or getting lost in your inbox compared to when you have vague idea about what to do or when you just wing it. Makes sense, right?

One of the best ways to always have clear goals is to make them **SMART**. This will transform your fuzzy destination from "somewhere north" to "123 Success Street" in your brain's GPS.

Here's what makes a goal SMART:

Specific	X "I want to focus better" √ "I will complete one task without checking my phone for 45 minutes"
Measurable	X "I'll work more efficiently" √ "I'll track my focused work sessions, aiming for four 45-minute blocks each day"
Achievable	X "I'll never get distracted again" √ "I'll reduce my daily social media checks from 20 to 5 during work hours"
Relevant	X "I should meditate because everyone does it" √ "I will practice 5 minutes of mindful breathing to improve my focus during meetings"
Time-bound	X "I'll get better at focusing eventually" √ "By the end of this month, I will establish a routine of three focused work blocks daily"

To have a better idea how this could look like in real-life. Let's say you've got a project report breathing down your neck. Instead of panicking, let's SMART-ify it:

Specific	X "I need to finish the report" ✓ "Complete a 10-page report including data analysis, recommendations, and conclusion"
Measurable	X "I'll work on it regularly" ✓ "Complete intro by Monday, data analysis by Wednesday, conclusions by Friday"
Achievable	X "I'll write it all in one day" ✓ "Dedicate two focused hours daily to report writing"
Relevant	X "I'm doing this because I have to!" ✓ "This report impacts our project's success and my performance review"
Time-bound	X "I'll finish it soon" ✓ "Submit completed report by 5 PM Friday"

When you transform your goals from vague wishes into SMART targets, you're essentially giving your brain perfect coordinates. No more mental wandering – you've got a destination locked in, and your focus knows exactly where to shine its light without bouncing everywhere.

Managing Priorities

Not all tasks deserve equal attention – just like not all emails need an immediate response. Prioritization is your first line of defense in managing your focus, helping you decide what truly deserves your attention now versus later.

Enter the Eisenhower Matrix (EM), a powerful tool named after President Dwight D. Eisenhower, who wisely observed, "What is important is seldom urgent and what is urgent is seldom important." This matrix helps you sort tasks into four distinct quadrants - based on how important, and how quickly they need to be done. Here how it works:

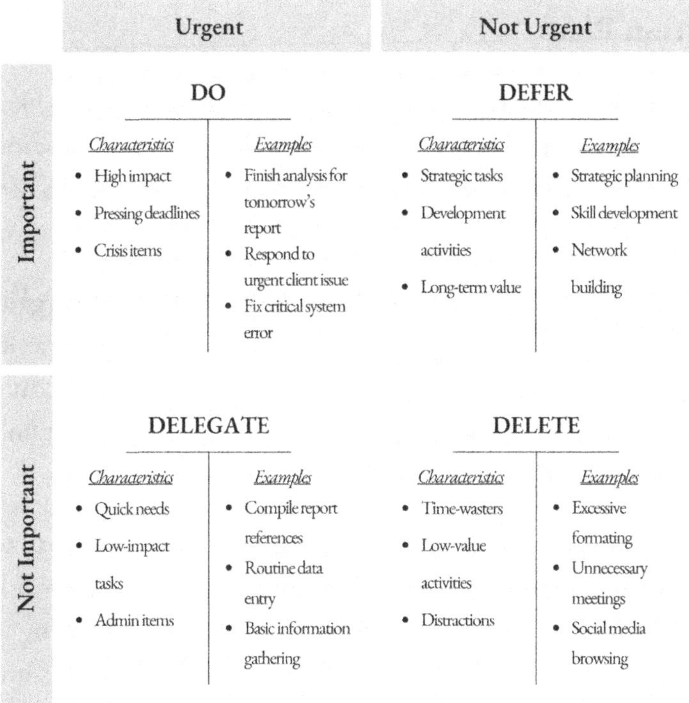

Let's see this in action with our report-writing scenario:

Priority Level	Tasks	Reasoning
DO FIRST	• Complete data analysis • Write core findings	Forms foundation of report (i.e. crucial for deadline)
SCHEDULE	• Design presentation • Draft recommendations	Important but can wait until main content is done
DELEGATE	• Reference compilation • Basic formatting	Urgent but others can handle
ELEMINATE	• Perfect font selection • Excessive visual design	Not crucial for report quality

Remember: Prioritization isn't just about knowing what to do – it's about knowing what **not** to do. When you focus on what truly matters, you'll find your mental energy stays stronger throughout the day.

Execution Plan

Having clear priorities is great, but without a solid plan, you're like a driver with a perfect destination but no GPS – you'll likely take some wrong turns along the way. That's where execution planning comes in. It turns your priorities into actionable steps, mapping out the fastest route to your goal.

Breaking down your work into detailed steps does more than organize tasks – it eliminates that paralyzing "where do I start?" feeling. With a clear plan, you'll spend less mental energy deciding what to do next because those decisions are already made. Think of it as freeing up your brain's RAM to focus purely on the task at hand.

The magic lies in the details: assigning specific time slots for each work chunk creates clear expectations about when things will happen, required resources identified upfront prevents those frustrating mid-task interruptions when you realize something's missing. Also, it's important to set regular checkpoints to track your progress and maintain momentum - there's nothing quite like seeing how far you've come to motivate you to keep going - just like having a GPS that not only shows your route but also tells you when to refuel and how far you've traveled.

Let's map this out for our report writing example:

Time Block	Task	Resources Needed	Expected Outcome
Day 1 - Morning	• Collect data • Initial Analysis	• Database access • Analysis software	• All data gathered • Key patterns identified
Day 1 - Afternoon	• Analyze findings • Draft outline	• Previous reports • Style guide	• Main points identified • Structure created
Day 2 - Morning	• Write core sections • Create graphs	• Writing software • Graphing tools	• Main content drafted • Visual aids ready
Day 2 - Afternoon	• Edit content • Finalize format	• Editing checklist • Format template	• Polished draft • Ready for review

Ration Out Your Focus

Sometimes tackling complex tasks can feel like trying to eat a whole cake in one bite – overwhelming and likely to cause indigestion. Dealing with large tasks can quickly drain your mental battery, and you'll need a strategy to maintain your focus throughout. Maintaining full concentration for extended periods is tough – that's where strategic chunking comes in handy. Think of it as eating that cake one calculated bite at a time, with small breaks to truly savor each piece.

The "*Pomodoro Technique*," named after the Italian word for "tomato" (inspired by a tomato-shaped kitchen timer), offers a proven rhythm of focus-intensive work and refreshing breaks – like interval training for your brain. While the classic format is 25 minutes of work with 5-minute breaks, followed by a longer break after four sessions, you can adjust this to your rhythm. For instance, some prefer 90/20 splits for long creative intervals, while others (myself included) find 40-minute focused sessions with 5-minute breaks more effective.

Here's how a day could look using 40-minute chunks with our report-writing example:

Time Block	Duration	Activity	Break Type
8:00 - 8:40	40 min	Understand scope and requirements	
8:40 - 8:45	5 min		Stand, and stretch
8:45 - 9:25	40 min	Gather relevant data	
9:25 - 9:30	5 min		Quick walk
9:30 - 10:10	40 min	Sort and organize data	
10:10 - 10:15	5 min		Eye exercises
10:15 - 10:55	40 min	Start analysis, identify patterns	
10:55 - 11:10	15 min		Longer movement break

11:10 - 11:50	40 min	Continue analysis	
11:50 - 11:55	5-10 min		Hydration and stretching
12:00 - 12:40	40 min	Complete findings, key points	
12:40 - 14:00	80 min		Lunch break
14:00 - 14:40	40 min	Draft report summary	
14:40 - 14:45	5 min		Stand and move
14:45 - 15:25	40 min	Ensure key points are explained	
15:25 - 15:30	5 min		Quick walk
15:30 - 16:10	40 min	Review and fine-tune	

Let's do the math: with this schedule, you get 6 hours and 40 minutes of pure focus-intensive work while taking just 50 minutes of short breaks (not counting lunch). That's 85-90% of your day in focus mode – but in manageable, energized chunks rather than one continuous drain. So, would you rather push through non-stop and hit a mental dip, or stay sharp all day with these strategic pauses?

To make the most of your focus-intensive work intervals, consider using a physical timer or an offline app to avoid the temptation of digital distractions[1] . During breaks, resist the urge to check your phone or scroll through social media - instead, use this time to move around, which will naturally boost your alertness. Stay hydrated, and adjust your work intervals based on your task's complexity and your energy levels. Remember: these aren't rigid rules but guidelines. The key is finding your optimal rhythm that keeps you productive without burning out.

1. I personally use an offline app called "Focus-To-Do" There are many similar apps available, choose one that works for your style and doesn't become a distraction itself.

Time Blocking: Organizing Your Focus Periods

Your daily energy fluctuates throughout the day, it's like a playlist that has high-energy tracks and slower, calmer ones. You can't maintain sustained focus all day, but you can arrange your tasks to match your natural energy patterns. Just as you wouldn't play energetic workout music during meditation, certain tasks fit better at specific times. The whole goal is to be able to arrange your focus periods strategically throughout the day.

For example, you could start your day with "focus-intensive" blocks when your energy is typically highest. This is the time for complex analysis, creative work, and strategic planning - activities like report writing, data analysis, and problem-solving that demand your sharpest thinking. As your day progresses and energy naturally dips to medium levels, shift to "light-processing" tasks. Mid-day is perfect for routine work like responding to emails, making basic updates, and handling light meetings - tasks that need attention but not intense concentration.

Late afternoon, when energy typically settles to medium-low levels, is ideal for "review and plan" type of work. Use this time for organizing, planning next steps, and reviewing progress - tasks that benefit from reflection but don't demand peak mental performance. Throughout your day, maintain "buffer zones" between these major blocks. These flexible periods handle unexpected tasks, transitions, and quick responses. Your energy might vary during these times, but that's okay - they're designed for urgent requests, short meetings, and quick decisions that inevitably pop up.

Here's how to integrate Pomodoro sessions within these blocks:

Time Period	Block Type	Pomodoro Structure	Activities
8:00 - 10:10	**Focus-intensive Work**	3 X 40-min sessions with 5-min breaks	• Report analysis • Complex problem-solving
10:10 - 10:30	**Buffer**	Extended break	• Transition time • Quick responses

10:30 - 12:40	Focus-intensive Work	3 X 40-min sessions with 5-min breaks	• Content creation • Strategic work
12:40 - 14:00	Recharge	Lunch break	• Rest and reset
14:00 - 15:30	Light-processing Work	2 X 40-min sessions with 5-min breaks	• Dealing with e-mails • Light tasks
15:30 - 16:30	Review & Plan	1 X 40-min session, and buffer time	• Day review • Tomorrow's plan

The key to successful time blocking lies in two core principles:

Energy Alignment: Match your toughest tasks to your peak energy periods. Pay attention to when you work best – morning person or night owl, plan accordingly.

Built-in Flexibility: Use the 80/20 rule instead of scheduling every minute. Plan about 80% of your time and leave 20% unscheduled. Those empty spaces aren't wasted time - they're breathing room for the unexpected things that always pop up during your day. This way, one surprise meeting or technical issue won't throw off your entire schedule. For example, in an 8-hour day, that's roughly 6.5 hours scheduled and 1.5 hours flexible. Think of it like leaving extra space in your suitcase – you'll probably need it![2]

Managing Transitions Between Blocks

The key to successful time blocking isn't just in the blocks themselves – it's in how you move between them. Think of transitions as your mental gear shifts. The most effective are those creating clear boundaries between work periods and involve physical or environmental changes. Here's how to handle them:

---

2. The great thing about the 80/20 rule is that it follows Parkinson's Law (work expands to fill available time) while acknowledging Murphy's Law (anything that can go wrong, will). So, this extra time should be fine to deal with the unexpected - urgent tasks, meeting overruns, and transition periods. This is the best way to avoid over-scheduling, which often leads to stress, rushed work, and a domino effect of delayed tasks when it happens.

Quick Resets (5 minutes): Perfect between Pomodoro sessions. Use this time for a quick stretch, a bathroom break, or simply resting your eyes. These short pauses help maintain your energy without breaking your workflow.

Standard Transitions (10-15 minutes): Use when switching between different time blocks. This is a buffer zone where you review completed work, and prepare for your next task. Serves as a mental reset to close one type of work properly before starting another.

Major Transitions (30 minutes): For significant shifts in your work. Change your environment, and include energy renewal activities[3] like short walks or stretching. A quick walk outside or change of scenery can do wonders for your mental reset – much better than scrolling through your phone!

Focus Protection System

Picture building a sandcastle on the beach – without protection from incoming waves, all your careful planning can wash away in seconds. The same goes for your focus time. It's crucial to defend your focus-intensive work periods when real life tries to interrupt. Those interruptions come in many forms: the digital deluge of emails and notifications, the colleague with a 'quick question' that's never quick, and even your environment with its sudden noises or temperature swings. But here's the good news – while you can't stop these interruptions completely (just like you can't stop the rain), a solid protection system acts like your focus umbrella, keeping your concentration dry and protected.

---

3. Energy renewal activities are just what they sound like - activities that actually recharge you, not drain you. This could be a short walk, some stretching, or even just looking out the window at nature. The key is to avoid things like social media that seem like breaks but actually tire you out more and deplete you mentally.

Interruption Prevention

Just as traffic lights manage vehicle flow, focus signals help control interruptions **before** they happen. They create a clear system that tells others when you're "in the zone" and when you're available for interaction - like 'headphones mean focus-intensive work, but tap my shoulder for urgent matter' or 'green light welcomes questions, red light means catch me later.' The goal isn't isolation, but creating a rhythm that helps everyone work better together. Here're some ideas on how to set up those signals:

Visual Signals

- Wear headphones (even without music) as a universal "Do Not Disturb" sign
- Use desk or door indicators (like red/green lights) to show availability – with - green means you're open to quick questions, red signals focus-demanding work time.

Digital Signals - **just as important as physical ones.**

- Block your focus periods in the shared calendar with your team.
- Set your status as "in focus-intensive mode" on communication platforms like Teams, or Slack.
- Enable auto-responses during focus-demanding work blocks.

The real power of focus signals lies in **clear**, **consistent** communication. Set specific focus hours (like 10 AM to 12 PM daily) and stick to them – your colleagues will quickly learn your rhythm. Many teams even implement meeting-free mornings, maximizing everyone's peak energy hours. But you have to communicate these boundaries professionally. Instead of a blunt 'I'm busy,' try 'I'm in a focus-intensive work block until 12, but I'd love to connect after lunch.' Explain to your colleagues how this system helps you deliver better work and be more present during collaborative times - you might say, "I'm working on being more intentional with my time so I can be more helpful when we do connect." Like this you'd maintain relationships while protecting your time.

Interruption Management

Even with strong focus signals, some interruptions will break through. However, when they do, having a clear protocol to handle them efficiently will get you back on track with minimal casualties. Here's how:

1. ***Pause:*** When interruption strikes, your first move is to save your current state. Mark where you are exactly stopping, like noting "stopping at data analysis section" or "next step: review third paragraph." This creates a mental bookmark for easy return.

2. ***Protect:*** Now that your work is safely paused, address the interruption with clear boundaries. This means first assess how urgent it is and set appropriate time limits. You might say "I can give this 5 minutes now" for truly urgent matters, or "Let's schedule time at 2PM" for things that can wait. As always, be clear, professional, and above all nice when you communicate your time boundaries.

3. ***Proceed:*** Returning back needs to be done gradually. Start with a quick reset (stretch, or breathe), then review where you left off. Finally start small and rebuild momentum to engage back in your full focus mode.

The success of your focus protection system lies in regular evaluation. When it's working well, this will lead to rare interruptions and people respecting your boundaries. If you notice frequent interruptions or boundary breaches, it's time to strengthen your prevention strategies. Similarly, your interruption management will be effective if it really helps you with smooth transitions and quick recovery to interrupted tasks. If you're struggling to regain focus or seeing productivity dips after interruptions, consider adjusting your recovery approach. Regular monitoring of these indicators helps you fine-tune your system for optimal protection of your most precious currency- time!

The Big Picture So Far...

Remember how we started – focus needs a clear destination, just like any journey you plan. Now we've built the high-performance engine to get you there. Every component plays a vital role: priorities guide your attention, clear plans break down big tasks, Pomodoro sessions maintain your energy, time blocks organize your day, and interruption strategies protect your focus. Like a well-oiled machine, these parts work in harmony.

But here's the catch – even with the perfect engine, what good is knowing your destination if you keep taking detours? What use is having a high-performance machine if you constantly override its optimal settings? That's our next challenge: transforming these strategies from tools you occasionally use into habits you naturally live by.

Activating Your Autopilot System

So far, every strategy we discussed requires conscious effort – like checking priorities, setting timers, or protecting time blocks. Wouldn't it be easier if they happened automatically? Remember learning to drive? Every action needed intense concentration at first. Now you probably check mirrors and signal without thinking twice. That's the power of habits. And while motivation might seem like enough, research shows that willpower is more like a muscle that eventually tires. Therefore, creating lasting change needs more than just determination.

Rooting out Focus-draining Habits

Remember our habit loop: cue, behavior, reward. Take phone checking – a notification sound (cue) leads to picking up your device (behavior) for that dopamine hit of new information received (reward). Understanding these patterns isn't about judgment; it's about recognition. Just like a gardener needs to know what's growing in their plot before pulling out harmful weed, you need to understand your habit patterns before changing them.

Let's examine the habits hijacking your focus. Think of them as background apps draining your phone's battery – you might not notice them running, but they're constantly sapping your mental energy. Here are the main culprits:

Digital Habits: Those are the sneakiest – like checking your phone without reason, reflexively opening email when you feel stuck, or taking that "quick peek" at social media that becomes an hour-long scroll.

Workspace Habits: Those create visual noise dividing your attention – like tolerating a messy desk because "you'll clean later", working in high-traffic areas, or keeping endless browser tabs open "just in case."

Work-related Habits: Those create false productivity feeling – like diving into tasks without planning, attempting to multitask when you know it doesn't work, or skipping breaks because you're "too busy."

Track Your Habit Patterns

To really understand what habits might be affecting your ability to focus, try breaking down your day and observing your patterns at different times. Think of this as creating a time-lapse of your day.

Morning Patterns - Your first hour often sets the day's tone, so pay good attention to what you do there. When do you first reach for your phone? How quickly do you check messages? What does the start of your workday actually look like? These early habits ripple through your entire day.

Peak Hours - During your productive time, what disrupts your flow? What breaks your concentration during focus-intensive work? How often do you jump between tasks?

Low Energy Periods - When tired, what's your go-to distraction? How do you respond to mental fatigue? What automatic behaviors emerge when you're tired? These default responses often reveal your most ingrained habits.

Again, the goal is not to judge these patterns but to notice them. Just as a doctor needs to know the symptoms to make an accurate diagnosis, you need this awareness to make effective changes.

Disrupting The Loop

Once you've mapped your habits, it's time to weaken their hold on your attention. Think of triggers as the first domino in your habit chain – knock it over, and the rest won't follow. By removing or altering these triggers, you start breaking the habit's spell. For instance, charging your phone in another room eliminates both evening and morning triggers for mindless checking– out of sight, out of mind.

For habits you can't completely avoid, add strategic friction – speed bumps that make you pause before the automatic response kicks in. For example:

Digital Habits

- Log out of email after each check.
- Remove social media apps or sign out after use.
- Turn off all but most critical notifications.
- Launch chat apps manually instead of auto-start.

- Use mindful pause apps that create a moment of reflection before scrolling.[4]

Workspace Habits

- Use bookmarks instead of keeping countless tabs open.
- Clear visual clutter from your workspace.

Each of these steps adds a small moment of conscious decision-making to what was previously automatic. The goal isn't making habits impossible, but turning them from mindless to intentional.

Replacing With Better

Sometimes disruption alone isn't enough – you need to replace the old habit with a better one. This works because it addresses the underlying need that created the habit in the first place.

First, understand your habit's true nature - why it exists and persists? You could ask:

- When does it typically show up?
- What triggers it?
- What emotional state precedes it?
- What need is it really fulfilling?

For instance, that reflexive phone check might happen when you're stuck on a difficult task. Is it giving you a mental break? Connection? Stress relief? Once you understand the real need, you can design better alternatives:

4. One sec app or similar apps.

Better Swaps

- Replace phone checks with quick stretch routines – you get your break plus physical benefits.
- Swap endless email checking for scheduled check times – maintaining both control and productivity.
- Trade social media scrolling for planned social time – real connection with proper boundaries.
- Replace tab hoarding with a solid note-taking system – staying organized without missing anything, and without the clutter.

After all, the goal isn't to deny your needs, but to meet them in ways that support rather than sabotage your focus.

The Recovery Journey

Like any significant change, breaking old habits follows a predictable pattern. Let's explore what to expect and how to navigate each stage.

First Few Days: Managing Withdrawal

Expect strong resistance at first – your brain will signal powerful urges to return to old patterns. This critical period is when most people either stay firm or slip back. You'll likely face three main challenges:

Digital FOMO: When anxiety about missing updates kicks in, combat it with structured check-in times. For instance, check emails at 10AM and 4PM only, review Slack messages at lunch, and save social media for end of day.

Task-Switching Urges: When you feel antsy and struggle to stay focused on one task. Counter this by using a timer for minimum focus periods, then gradually increase duration as your focus muscle strengthens.

Dopamine Cravings: When you feel that restless craving quick stimulation, replace the dopamine digital hit with meaningful rewards - maybe a coffee after completing a focus block, or music during breaks. Break work into micro-achievements and cross them off- even if this is to finish a block of 10-15 minutes of uninterrupted focus. These tiny wins provide immediate, tangible satisfaction replacing the digital rewards your brain is used to.

The Path Forward

As you move into week one, your initial impulses decrease - you start recognizing patterns. That's your brain beginning to accept the new normal, though it's still testing boundaries.

By the second week and beyond- new patterns solidify, withdrawal symptoms fade, and focus capacity naturally increases. The benefits become more apparent, making it easier to maintain your new direction.

Growing Focus-Supporting Habits

Breaking free from focus-draining habits is just the first step. Like a gardener who doesn't only remove weeds but also plants flowers, we need to cultivate new habits that actively enhance our focus. Aristotle noted that 'Nature abhors a vacuum', and this is especially true for our minds - any empty space in our routine will get filled, either by old habits creeping back or new distractions taking root. That's why it's crucial to intentionally plant habits that make your focus ecosystem stronger.

Habit Stacking: Tiny Consistent Steps

Start incredibly small - so small it might seem trivial. Like stacking pennies, each tiny action compounds into substantial growth. For example:

- Begin by simply closing your laptop at day's end.

- Progress to setting tomorrow's priorities.
- Build up to a full routine of clearing your desk and prepping materials for next morning.

Even micro-habits matter: turning your phone face-down for 10 minutes can grow into established phone-free zones, and standing up once an hour can evolve into a complete break routine.

Piggybacking: Growing New Branches

Rather than creating entirely new routines – which is hard, attach (or piggyback) focus habits to existing ones – like adding new branches to a strong tree you already have in your habits garden. The strategy is simple: identify your reliable daily routines, add one small focus habit to each. For example:

- While waiting for your morning coffee to brew (existing habit) → Review daily priorities (new habit).
- Computer startup → Clear desk.
- Lunch break → Quick progress check.
- End-of-day routine → Set tomorrow's to-do list.

These natural transitions become perfect anchors to trigger your new focus habits - making them more likely to stick.

Habit Chains: Creating Natural Rhythms

Just as your morning bathroom routine flows without thought, you can create smooth focus sequences throughout your day. Once small habits take root, link them together to turn into a well-choreographed dance – each move naturally leading to the next. The created rhythms will eliminate any fatigue from deciding what to do next.

Here's how to chain your focus habits:

Morning Launch: Computer on → Set up workspace → Review priorities → Prep what you need in your first focus session – creates momentum for the day.

Focus Block Start: Clear desk → Set timer → Activate "Do Not Disturb" signals - creates your personal focus bubble.

Break Time: Stretch → Hydrate → Prep next task - maintains energy flow.

Mid-day Reset: Tidy space before going for lunch → Update task list → Adjust plans (if needed) - sets up strong afternoon session for when you're back.

End-day Wrap: Save work → Review accomplishments → Prep tomorrow → Clear space - ensures a fresh start the next day.

These chains are flexible templates – adapt them to your natural rhythm and work style. You'll know they're effective when one action flows seamlessly cuing the next - creating an effortless focus dance through your day.

Tracking and Troubleshooting

What gets measured gets improved. So, tracking your focus habits is crucial because it shows you what's actually working versus what you think is working. Without measurement, you're just guessing. Plus, seeing your progress, creates motivation by making your habit-building efforts concrete and visible. Also, this same tracking system becomes your early warning detector when habits start to wobble, helping you spot and fix issues before they grow into bigger problems.

Simple Tracking System

- Use a basic checkmark system for daily habits.

- Note both habit completion and how well you did.
- Monitor key routines like: Morning priority reviews – Focus block completions – Break routine consistency – Energy levels throughout the day.

Your tracking system should be simple enough to maintain but detailed enough to spot patterns. Like a car's dashboard, it shouldn't distract from the driving – it should just help you stay on course.

When Things Get Bumpy

Even well-tracked habits can stumble. Don't worry, it's a normal part of the process. When they do, don't try fixing everything all at once. Return to basics, and make the first step impossibly small. Simplify your routines - three tiny consistent steps beat ten ambitious ones. You could also consider sharing your goals with a friend to help you stay accountable.

Remember to keep solutions simple and always focus on progress, not perfection. Your focus habits need constant, gentle tending rather than occasional dramatic changes.

Putting It All Together: The Complete Picture

We started the chapter with the intention of building a high-performance focus engine. Now all the components are in place: SMART goals and priorities serve as your navigation system, pointing you in the right direction. Time management acts as your fuel injection, ensuring energy flows to the right tasks at the right time. Your protection strategies work like the engine's cooling system, preventing overheating from distractions. And habits? They're your automatic transmission, making the whole system run smoothly without constant manual adjustment.

Each component strengthens the others – clear goals guide habit formation, strong habits improve time management, and good time management creates space for meaningful work. While it takes initial effort to assemble, once running, this engine turns focus-intensive work mode into your default setting, carrying you smoothly toward your destinations.

12

Full Body Overhaul

"Your life doesn't get better by chance, it gets better by change." -Jim Rohn

Optimizing Your Focus

We've built a powerful focus engine with core skills. Now it's time to optimize the rest of your vehicle. Think about it: even the most advanced Formula 1 engine won't win races if it's sitting in a car with worn-out parts, running on low-grade fuel, or missing maintenance. Your focus skills are that engine—but they need comprehensive support from everything else under the hood.

Your body isn't just a collection of parts—it's an integrated performance machine. Your lunch choices affect your afternoon focus, your sleep quality influences next-day decision-making, and that morning workout might be your best defense against mental fatigue. When these elements work together, they create a powerful foundation for sustained attention.

The Two Pillars of Peak Performance:

1. **Physical Foundation**: This is your ***hardware*** setup. Just like any machine needs the right components to run smoothly, your body needs proper nutrition, quality sleep, and strategic movement to maintain peak cognitive performance. Research shows that even modest improvements in these areas can significantly enhance focus.

2. **Mental Resilience**: Consider this your ***operating system***. It's the software that helps you handle stress, manage emotions, and maintain focus under pressure. Studies show that people with strong mental resilience can maintain focus for longer during challenging tasks.

You don't need to become a health guru to optimize your body for better focus. The big difference usually comes from tiny improvements that compound with time. Ready to fine-tune your focus machine? Let's start with your hardware then.

Nutrition

Picture your brain as a race car driver, making split-second decisions and executing intricate maneuvers throughout the day. Remarkably, while your brain accounts for only 2% of your body weight, it requires an astonishing 20% of your total energy! Just as a top driver needs high-quality fuel at precisely the right moments, your brain requires optimal nutrition to maintain peak performance. After all, you wouldn't send an elite driver onto the track with low-grade fuel, or would you?!

The Winning Strategy

Sometimes one feels sharp and focused after certain meals, but sluggish and unfocused after others. Well, that's not a coincidence! Research indicates that to optimize your mealtimes, you need to focus on three key aspects: timing, quality, and how you eat.

When to Fuel Up

Consuming a protein-rich breakfast within an hour of waking up can help you maintain focus for up to 4 hours longer compared to skipping breakfast or only eating carbohydrates. For lunch, eat before you become extremely hungry to prevent overeating, and tackle your most challenging tasks before lunch when your energy levels are naturally at their peak. Sustain your focus throughout the day with strategically timed, nutrient-dense snacks to bridge potential energy dips.

What to Put in Your Tank

Your brain's performance is greatly influenced by the nutrients you provide. Nutrient-rich foods like omega-3 rich fish, antioxidant-packed berries, complex carbohydrates like quinoa, and lean proteins from eggs and legumes act as premium fuel for your brain. On the other hand, sugary, fatty, or heavily processed foods can hinder your focus by causing energy crashes and mental fatigue.

Refined sugars cause rapid spikes in blood sugar, followed by sharp crashes that can leave you feeling tired and foggy. Heavy, fatty meals divert blood flow away from your brain to aid in digestion, leading to a temporary decrease in cognitive function. Processed foods often lack essential nutrients and can promote inflammation, which has been linked to impaired brain function. Conversely, whole, nutrient-dense foods provide a steady supply of energy and vital nutrients to support optimal brain function.

To maintain stable energy levels, it's essential to balance your blood sugar - consider it your brain's fuel gauge. Strive for meals consisting of 40% complex carbohydrates, 30% lean protein, and 30% healthy fats. Begin your day with protein and healthy fats, keep your lunch portions moderate, and make informed snack choices every 3-4 hours. Think of snacks as high-performance fuel top-ups to keep you going strong.

Mindful Eating

Your meal breaks are crucial pit stops in your focus race. Avoid consuming lunch quickly while scrolling through your phone – that's a major focus disruptor. Distracted eating leads to overeating, rushed meals, and digestive issues. Besides, scrolling through social media while eating can deplete dopamine levels, making it more challenging to focus later on. It's a double hit for your performance - your body struggles to properly process the fuel while your brain gets mentally drained.

Instead, treat mealtime as a real break - a true transition point in your day. Move away from the screen and savor your food mindfully. Even better, engage in conversation with colleagues - a little lunchtime chat can refresh your mind while you nourish your body. When you return to work, you'll be operating at your best, rather than struggling with a post-lunch energy dip.

Hydration

Just like a race car needs proper cooling to maintain peak performance, your brain requires optimal hydration to function at its best. In fact, even a mild 2% decrease in hydration can lead to a significant drop in cognitive performance. It's time to give your brain the cooling it needs to keep you focused and sharp.

To keep your brain running smoothly, start your day by drinking 2 cups of water within an hour of waking up. Rather than chugging large amounts at once, sip consistently throughout the day to maintain steady hydration levels. About 30 minutes before diving into focus-demanding work, drink another cup of water to give your brain an extra boost.

Making Hydration a Habit

Staying hydrated doesn't have to be a chore. Make it easier by keeping water visible - simply having a water bottle in sight can increase your consumption. Use a marked bottle to track your intake and set regular hydration reminders to keep yourself on track. Soon, reaching for water will become second nature, and your brain will thank you for it.

Fueling Your Focus

Remember, every food and drink choice you make is either an investment in or a withdrawal from your focus account. Your brain doesn't just need fuel - it needs the right fuel, consumed at the right times and in the right way. Prioritizing hydration alongside strategic nutrition will give your brain the comprehensive support it needs to keep you at the top of your game.

Sleep: Brain's Essential Reset

Sleep is your brain's ultimate recharge station - more powerful than any energy drink or supplement. Sleep not only provides physical rest but, most importantly, it gives your brain the time it needs to process, repair, and prepare for peak performance. Research shows that just one poor night's sleep can significantly impair your reaction time and slash your focus ability the next day. It's like trying to win a race with only half your engine functioning.

But it's not just about logging hours in bed - it's about the quality of the sophisticated maintenance cycles happening under the hood. Every night, your brain runs through four to six of these cycles, each lasting about 90 minutes. Think of each cycle as a complete washing machine program, with three distinct phases:

1. **Light Sleep** (50%): This is your system's basic maintenance mode. Your heart rate slows, body temperature drops, and muscles relax while maintaining some responsiveness to your environment.

2. **Deep Sleep** (20%): Consider this your body's major repair phase. This is when your body shifts into high gear, focusing on tissue growth and repair, bone and muscle building, and immune system strengthening.

3. **REM Sleep** (30%): During REM (Rapid Eye Movement) sleep, your brain files away the day's experiences, converting short-term memories into long-term storage and forming new neural connections, enhancing learning and problem-solving abilities.

The percentage of time spent in each phase isn't random - it's your body's optimized formula for complete restoration. What's fascinating is how your body orchestrates this nightly maintenance schedule. Between 10 PM and 2 AM, when melatonin production peaks, your body prioritizes physical repairs. Then, from 2 AM until sunrise, as melatonin levels gradually decrease, the focus shifts to brain maintenance, processing data and clearing mental clutter. That's why a good night's sleep can often bring clarity to issues that seemed overwhelming the night before, and why you may wake up feeling refreshed and more positive. That's your brain's night crew doing quality work during these crucial hours.

Optimizing Sleep Quality

When it comes to sleep, quality trumps quantity - six hours of high-quality rest can be more restorative than eight hours of poor sleep. To optimize your sleep quality, you'll need to fine-tune a few critical elements working in harmony: your environment, your timing, and your daily habits.

Creating the Perfect Sleep Environment

Your sleep environment's temperature should be in the optimal range of 65-68°F (18-20°C) - your body's preferred setting for deep sleep. Ensure complete darkness to support natural melatonin production, and maintain either perfect silence or consistent white noise to prevent disruptive sound fluctuations. Good air circulation isn't just for comfort; it's essential for maintaining optimal sleep conditions throughout the night.

Timing Your Sleep and Wake Cycles

Think of waking up like catching the perfect wave - you want to align with your body's natural sleep cycles. By waking at the end of a complete 90-minute cycle, you're more likely to feel refreshed rather than groggy. Within 15 minutes of waking, expose yourself to bright light - it's like hitting your brain's "power on" switch.

For those needing mid-day recharging, strategic napping can serve as a performance booster. However, it requires precise timing:

- A *power nap* (10-20 minutes) before 3 PM can boost cognitive performance for up to 3 hours after waking up.
- A *full recovery nap* (90 minutes) allows completion of a full sleep cycle.

Naps between 30 and 90 minutes often lead to sleep inertia - that groggy, disoriented state that leaves you feeling worse than before. This happens because you're interrupting your brain during deep sleep, rather than letting it complete its natural cycle. It's like stopping a washing machine mid-cycle - you'll neither get the benefit of a quick rinse nor a complete wash.

If you need more than a power nap, commit to the full 90 minutes to ensure your brain completes its entire sleep cycle. This is particularly important for shift workers or when making up for sleep debt.

Establishing Sleep-Supporting Habits

Just as professional athletes maintain strict pre-game routines, your sleep pattern should be consistent - even on weekends. This consistency helps your body's internal clock maintain its precision timing, much like keeping a high-performance engine properly tuned.

The most essential habit to improve your sleep quality is a "*digital sunset*" routine – gradually reducing and eventually eliminating exposure to digital screens (phones, tablets, computers) 1-2 hours before bedtime. The blue light these devices emit can interfere with your body's natural melatonin production, disrupting any chance of a good night's sleep. This digital wind-down is crucial to signal to your brain to begin its natural sleep preparation process.

Don't overlook your morning launch, which should include exposure to natural light, hydration, and gentle movement – this is your system's proper startup sequence. Throughout the day, maintain sleep-supporting habits that will help your body get ready for sleep at night, such as monitoring caffeine intake (cutting off after 2 PM), exercising regularly (but not close to bedtime), and managing your light exposure strategically.

Optimizing your sleep environment, timing your sleep and wake cycles, and establishing consistent sleep-supporting habits will ensure your brain gets the high-quality rest it needs to perform at its best.

Movement: Organic Focus Booster

Ever felt foggy after sitting for too long? That's not just your body craving a stretch - it's your brain sending an urgent message to get moving! Exercise isn't just a physical tune-up; it's your brain's natural focus-enhancing drug.

Research shows that regular physical activity (PA) can significantly boost your cognitive performance and sharpen your attention.

In our world of constant digital distractions, social media scrolling, and endless notifications, our brain's reward system gets hijacked. Each like, comment, and retweet triggers a small dopamine hit, gradually depleting our natural focus abilities. It's like being stuck on a mental hamster wheel, constantly seeking the next quick fix.

Here's where the magic of movement comes in. Physical activity acts as a powerful reset button for your brain. It naturally boosts dopamine production and helps rewire your brain's reward system, making it easier to find satisfaction in deep, focused work rather than fleeting digital distractions. Regular exercise can indeed help reverse the dopamine depletion caused by excessive screen time and social media use, allowing you to break free from the digital distraction cycle.

Strategic Movement

Think of movement as your brain's natural coffee - timing is everything. Morning movement increases alertness, setting a positive momentum for the day. Midday movement breaks up extended sitting periods and combats the afternoon slump, serving as a mental reset. Evening exercise, which should focus on light movement to avoid disrupting sleep patterns, is the best way to reduce the day's stress.

Your Perfect Prescription

There's a big movement pharmacy out there, with each type of exercise offering unique benefits for your brain, allowing you to choose the right "prescription" for your needs. Cardio activities like running, cycling, or swimming provide immediate focus boosts and can increase your

BDNF (brain-derived neurotrophic factor) by up to 3 times[1]. BDNF is like a superfood for your brain helping it to stay sharp and learn better. Resistance training improves executive function for a few hours post-workout, while mindful movements like yoga and tai chi clear your mind and enhance concentration.

Intensity

Intensity is an important factor in your movement prescription. *High-intensity* (*HI*) workouts (20-30 minutes, 2-3 times weekly) are best for dopamine reset and morning energy. *Moderate-intensity* (*MI*) sessions (30-45 minutes, 3-4 times weekly) support sustained focus and can be done anytime. *Low-intensity* (*LI*) movement (10-15 minutes, daily) helps maintain mental clarity and can be spread throughout the day.

Integration

Integrate movement strategically into your workday with stand-up work sessions or walking meetings.[2] Match exercise type to your focus needs - light movement, like movement snacks[3], during short breaks, and recovery activities, like gentle stretching, after intense focus periods.

---

1. You know that famous "Miracle-Gro" fertilizer that you just sprinkle it on, and plants tend to flourish? BDNF is quite similar. It's what the brain cells need to make sure they stay healthy, grow new connections, and adapt to new information more easily. That's why exercise isn't just good for your body – it's literally feeding your brain what it needs to thrive!

2. Walking meetings involve discussing agenda items while walking together, instead of sitting in a conference room, or using an under-desk treadmill during virtual meetings. They are suitable for one-on-one or small group discussions, brainstorming sessions, or informal catch-ups.

3. Movement snacks are brief 2-5 minute bursts of physical activity strategically spread throughout your day. Rather than trying to compensate for 8 hours of sitting with a single workout, these short movement breaks help to maintain your body's natural rhythm and keep your brain energized without requiring a change of clothes or leaving you exhausted. Examples include desk stretches, standing exercises, walking, simple mobility work, and basic yoga poses.

Start small and build gradually, beginning with 5-minute movement snacks from the comfort of your seat. Track your energy levels to find your optimal pattern. Regular movement provides the right maintenance routine for your focus machine - it's not just about fitness, it's about optimizing your brain's performance. Find your personal sweet spot in timing, type, and intensity to best support your focus rhythm.

Physical activity isn't just good for your body - it's your brain's natural focus booster. Every movement, from a brisk walk to a full workout, sharpens your attention. So next time your focus wanes, skip the coffee and digital distractions - give your brain the movement it craves. Your enhanced productivity will be worth it.

Efficient Energy Usage: Harness Your Natural Rhythm

Now that you've optimized your hardware components, let's focus on the peaks and valleys your energy levels naturally experience throughout the day - which can make or break your focus. Most people have their primary surge of energy between 9-11 AM and an afternoon revival from 3-5 PM, with natural dips occurring after lunch (1-3 PM) and in the evening. However, these patterns vary based on your personal chronotype - your body's unique rhythm.

Discovering Your Energy Pattern

To discover your distinct energy pattern, keep an energy journal for a week, rating your levels hourly on a scale of 1-10. This will help you better understand the natural distribution of your energy throughout the day. With this knowledge, you can master the art of matching your tasks to your energy levels, working with your body's natural rhythm instead of against it.

Matching Tasks to Your Energy Levels

During peak hours, tackle complex problem-solving, creative work, and important decisions. Use medium-energy periods for routine tasks, team meetings, and administrative work. Reserve low-energy times for simple organization, planning, and review tasks. By aligning your activities with your energy levels, you'll optimize your productivity and minimize burnout.

Recharging Your Energy

Effective energy management isn't about forcing your system to run on empty - it's about optimizing your natural power cycles. Be kind to your body and help it conserve and regenerate energy to ensure maximum performance. When you feel your energy starting to waver during a time block of focus-intensive work, take a 5-minute energy break to reset your posture and practice deep breathing.

For a longer breather to recharge your energy after an intense focus block, consider taking a meal break, a power nap, or spending time in nature. These simple strategies can work wonders for your energy levels when implemented consistently in your daily routine.

Unlock Your Full Potential

Work smarter by aligning your activities with your natural energy patterns. When you match tasks to your body's rhythm, you'll accomplish more with less effort and stress. It's that simple.

Mental Resilience: Your Performance OS

Having built our foundation through physical optimization, it's time to focus on the software that runs your focus machine. Think of mental resilience as your operating system—the sophisticated software that integrates all components and ensures they work together effectively. Just as a computer needs a robust OS to process data and maintain stability, your mind needs a strong system to manage cognitive and emotional challenges while maintaining focus.

Your mental resilience OS can be upgraded through experience and training. Each time you successfully navigate a challenging situation, you strengthen this system. Like software updates that improve performance, these experiences enhance your ability to handle stress, regulate emotions, and maintain focus under pressure.

This resilience isn't about avoiding challenges—it's about processing them effectively. A well-trained mental OS helps you adapt to changing circumstances, maintain emotional balance, and sustain focus even in demanding situations. Most importantly, it protects your focus system from being derailed by stress, pressure, or unexpected obstacles.

In the following sections, we'll go over specific strategies to upgrade your mental resilience. These practical tools will help you build a robust operating system that supports and enhances your focus capabilities.

Managing Stress: Your Mental CTRL+ALT+DEL

Just as your computer needs restart protocols, your mental operating system needs efficient ways to process stress and reset focus. Research shows that even five minutes of these mental reboot features can lead to measurable stress reduction and improved concentration.

Mindful Micro-Meditations - *Basic System Scan*

Start with two-minute micro-meditations—think of these as your quick system diagnostic. Find a comfortable position, close your eyes if possible, and simply count each inhale and exhale for just 120 seconds. This brief pause acts like hitting CTRL+ALT+DEL in your brain, clearing your mental cache and resetting your focus. The beauty of micro-meditations lies in their flexibility—you can practice them anywhere: at your desk, during your commute, or even in a busy meeting. Use them between tasks, before important meetings, or whenever your mind feels overloaded.

Advanced Features

Once comfortable with basic micro-meditations, enhance their effectiveness with three powerful upgrades:

1. **Focus Point Selection** (*Attention Anchoring*[4]): Choose one specific sensation as your default reset point—your breathing, feet on the floor, or even background sounds. This becomes your go-to focus point, shifting your attention away from stressors. Think of it as setting a home screen on your phone; whenever stress or distraction hits, return to this familiar point. For instance, if breathing is your chosen focus point, you can do quick check-ins throughout the day just by noticing three full breaths. This should be fairly easy once you've mastered the two-minute micro-meditations.

2. **Present-Moment Awareness**: When stress triggers an urge for immediate action, switch to "observation mode" instead. Take 30 seconds to run a system check: notice tensed shoulders, racing thoughts, or building anxiety. This quick scan helps you read your body's status report before responding. You're not trying to fix anything—just gathering data about your current state. Such awareness will prevent you from taking any impulsive action.

3. **Mindful Transitions**: Before switching activities, take 30 seconds to mentally "save and close" your current task and prepare for the next one. This prevents the scattered feeling of carrying

---

4. Attention anchoring comes from the nautical metaphor of using an anchor to keep a ship steady. In mindfulness practice, it refers to selecting a consistent point of focus that serves as a stable reference point. Just as a ship's anchor prevents drifting in changing waters, an attention anchor helps maintain mental stability amid life's distractions.

unfinished thoughts between tasks. For example, before leaving a meeting, quickly note key points, take a deep breath, and mentally prepare for your next activity.

Remember: Consistency trumps duration. Regular brief check-ins prove more effective than occasional long sessions. Start with basic micro-meditations, then gradually incorporate these advanced features as they become comfortable.

Progressive Muscle Relaxation (PMR) - *Full-System Reboot*

Think of PMR as your body-mind reboot protocol—a comprehensive scan of your physical hardware that helps identify and release hidden tension. Like running a full diagnostic on your system, PMR systematically checks and resets each part of your body.

Basic Protocol

Find a quiet space where you can sit or lie down comfortably for about 10 minutes. Starting from your feet, you'll perform a systematic tension-and-release sequence, working your way up through each muscle group to your face. For each area:

1. **Tension phase**: Deliberately tense the muscle group for 5-7 seconds—enough to feel it clearly but not to cause pain.
2. **Release phase**: Suddenly let go and relax completely for 10-15 seconds, paying attention to the sensation of relaxation flowing into the muscles.

Quick Reset Options

Once familiar with the full basic protocol, you can implement mini-versions as quick resets throughout your day:

- *Desk reset*: Focus on shoulders, neck, and jaw for a 30-second tension-release cycle.

- *Pre-meeting reset*: Target legs, core, and shoulders.
- *Focus boost*: Target facial and neck muscles when concentration starts to slip.

Strategic Implementation

Think of PMR as regular maintenance for your body-mind system. Just as you wouldn't wait for your car's engine to fail before servicing it, use PMR consistently to prevent tension buildup:

- *Morning*: Start with a full sequence to set a baseline of relaxation.
- *Throughout day*: Use mini-resets, targeting areas where you personally hold tension.
- *Before challenges*: Implement quick sequences before difficult tasks or meetings.
- *Evening*: End with a full sequence to release accumulated tension.

With regular practice, you'll develop what's like an early alarm for stress. You'll start noticing tension patterns—like jaw clenching during difficult meetings or shoulder hunching when deadlines loom. These become your body's "check engine lights," signaling when you need to pause for a reset.

Breathing Protocols

Breathing exercises are among the most powerful ways to reduce stress and clear your mind. By modulating your autonomic nervous system responses, these techniques naturally decrease heart rate and respiratory rate—key indicators of stress reduction. Here are two proven techniques to help regulate your system's performance:

Stress Release Sigh

The simplest yet highly effective technique for immediate tension release. Take a deep inhale through your nose, followed by a second short inhalation to fill your lungs completely. Then, let your shoulders drop as you exhale slowly through your mouth. This acts as your emergency pressure valve when you need quick stress relief.

Box Breathing

Made famous by Navy SEALs[5] who incorporated this technique into their stress-management training program to maintain clarity during high-pressure operations. Box breathing creates a steady rhythm for your nervous system. Picture drawing a square with your breath:

- Inhale for 4 counts (up).
- Hold for 4 counts (across).
- Exhale for 4 counts (down).
- Hold for 4 counts (across).

This technique helps maintain composure under pressure and enhances focus during challenging tasks.

Alternative Rhythms

- *5-5 Breathing*: A simpler version without breath-holding. Inhale for 5 counts, exhale for 5 counts. Perfect for maintaining steady concentration or quickly returning to focus after distractions.
- *4-7-8 Breathing*: Ideal for deep relaxation. Inhale quietly for 4

---

5. Navy SEALs (Sea, Air, and Land) are a special operations force of the US Navy, known for their rigorous training, mental toughness, and ability to perform under extreme pressure.

counts, hold for 7, then exhale for 8 while making a "whoosh" sound. The extended exhalation activates your parasympathetic nervous system—your body's 'rest and digest' mode—essentially switching on your internal 'chill switch' that slows heart rate, relaxes muscles, and calms your mind. This makes it particularly effective for pre-sleep relaxation.

Remember: Like any skill, these protocols become more effective with practice. Start with one technique that matches your current needs, master it, then gradually expand your breathing toolkit.

Emotional Control

Just as your computer constantly monitors its internal state, your mental OS includes a sophisticated emotion sensor. Rather than trying to override or ignore these emotional readings, you can install programs that help you monitor and respond to them effectively. Research shows that proper emotional processing accelerates recovery time, helping you return to peak performance faster. Incorporating an emotional regulation tool into your mental OS will make you ready in the face of tough situations, maintaining stability with great resilience and adaptability.

Self-Awareness

Developing self-awareness is a crucial diagnostic tool to manage your emotions and optimize performance. Here are three key steps to help you better understand your emotions and their impact on your work:

1. *Identify your emotional triggers*: Start by noting down all external or internal triggers that affect your performance, such as specific situations, people, places, thoughts, memories, physical sensations, or even particular times of the day or week. Journaling is a useful tool for this – keeping a quick log of these triggers and your responses to them for a week can reveal surprising patterns or trends in your emotional reactions.

2. *Analyze the impact of emotions on your performance*: Once you've identified your triggers, perform some performance analytics. Assess how your overall work quality was affected by different emotional states. Track your initial reactions to situations, monitor the duration of various emotional states, observe how your responses affected your focus, and note which responses helped or hindered your performance.

3. *Monitor your energy-emotion connection*: Another important aspect to monitor is how your energy levels impact your emotional responses and vice versa. For example, you might discover that low energy at 3 PM often leads to frustration or that anxiety tends to drain your energy faster than other emotions. By understanding this connection, you can match daily tasks to your optimal energy-emotion states, saving analytical work during high-energy, calm states and creative tasks during medium-energy, positive moods.

Additionally, keep track of your recovery time after emotional events and learn how long you need to recover from different emotional states. Note the best recovery methods for various situations – you might find that a 10-minute walk resets both energy and emotions better than a coffee break.

After all, the goal isn't to eliminate emotions but to use this awareness as an early warning system, helping you maintain stability and performance even when conditions get challenging.

Pressure Coping

Research shows that how we perceive pressure directly affects our performance. People who learn to view stress as "performance-enhancing" consistently outperform those who see it as purely negative. While there are many pressure-management strategies—like deep breathing, brief walks, or talking with trusted colleagues—***cognitive reframing*** stands out as one of the most powerful tools for transforming how we handle challenging situations.

Upgrade Your Mental Approach

Reframing transforms your relationship with pressure by shifting from a 'victim' mindset that feels trapped by circumstances to a 'survivor' mindset that sees opportunities for growth and adaptation. Consider how victim language keeps you stuck in patterns of helplessness: 'My team always dumps last-minute work on me,' 'I'm terrible at public speaking,' or 'This project is too overwhelming.' This mindset narrows your perspective and drains your energy, making every challenge feel like a threat to your performance.

In contrast, survivor language opens up possibilities and puts you back in control – moving you from the passenger seat to the driver's seat of your own experience. Instead of saying 'I have to deal with this impossible deadline,' try 'I'm choosing to demonstrate my ability to prioritize effectively.' Rather than 'This presentation is going to be stressful,' shift to 'I'm excited to showcase the preparation I've invested in.' When you catch yourself thinking 'Everyone else seems to handle pressure better than me,' reframe it as 'I'm discovering my own strategies for performing under pressure.'

Applying Reframing

Reframing becomes particularly powerful in daily work situations. When faced with a challenging project, the victim mindset might say 'This is way too complex; I'll never figure it out.' The survivor mindset transforms this into 'This project gives me a chance to develop new problem-solving skills.' When receiving critical feedback, instead of 'My boss never appreciates my work,' try 'I'm gathering valuable insights to enhance my performance.'

The key lies in expanding your perspective – taking a wide-angle view of each situation. Ask yourself: Will this matter in a month? What skills am

I developing through this challenge? What opportunities for growth am I discovering? This approach transforms "overwhelming problems" into "intriguing puzzles to solve," shifting from 'Why is this happening to me?' to 'What can I learn from this?'

Remember, reframing isn't about denying challenges – it's about approaching them with a mindset that empowers rather than diminishes you. Each time you catch yourself using victim language, pause and consciously shift to survivor language. With practice, this resilient thinking style becomes your default mode, helping you maintain peak performance even under pressure.

Don't Jump The Gun

Sometimes the best emotional response is no immediate response at all. Installing a deliberate pause—an emergency brake system—can prevent impulsive decisions and irrational actions. This simple but powerful tool starts with a 10-second pause before responding to triggering situations, creating valuable breathing space between emotion and reaction.

Start by practicing the pause during low-stakes situations (like email responses) to gradually build the habit for when you really need it. Practice evaluating any tough situation systematically, map out different response options, and potential outcomes of each response. For instance, when feeling overwhelmed by more work assigned to you by your boss, pause to consider, and ask yourself: "can I delegate? delay? decline? or need to deliver?"

The more you practice this pause protocol, the more natural it becomes, helping you maintain an unwavering emotional state in increasingly challenging situations.

Unshakeable Resilience

Just as any high-performance operating system requires regular maintenance and thoughtful upgrades, your mental resilience needs consistent attention. The tools we've explored—from mindfulness meditation and PMR to breathing protocols and emotional regulation strategies—aren't just quick fixes. They're core components of a robust mental operating system designed to handle whatever challenges come your way.

The goal isn't to create a system that never faces challenges—that's like trying to build a car that never needs maintenance. Instead, we're developing a responsive and resilient system that can: handle various conditions, adapt to challenges, recover quickly from any performance dips, and maintain stability under pressure.

As you practice these techniques consistently, you'll notice your mental OS becoming increasingly responsive and reliable. The beauty lies in its customization—you can adjust and fine-tune these programs to match your specific needs and circumstances. Start small, be patient with the installation process, and watch as your mental operating system transforms into a powerful ally in your journey toward sustained excellence.

Putting It All Together

We began this chapter with a mission to optimize your entire focus system - not just the engine we built earlier, but every component that supports and enhances it. Now the full machine is ready: your physical foundation serves as the chassis, with strategic nutrition fueling performance and quality sleep providing essential maintenance. Movement acts as your natural turbocharger, boosting mental clarity and resetting your dopamine system. Your energy management serves as the transmission, smoothly shifting between different performance needs throughout the day.

Crowned by your mental resilience operating system, this complete package doesn't just handle daily challenges - it transforms them into opportunities for growth. While the initial setup requires attention, once these components work in harmony, they create a self-sustaining cycle of peak performance, making sustained focus your natural state rather than a constant struggle.

13

Focus Feng Shui

"Outer order contributes to inner calm."
-Gretchen Rubin

Focus-friendly Spaces

After putting together the screws and bolts of your focus engine, and optimizing the hardware and software with premium components, it's time to create the perfect track for your high-performance Focus vehicle. Because even the most perfectly tuned cars need the right road conditions to show what it can really do. Attempting to focus in a chaotic environment is like trying to drive your carefully-assembled car through a muddy road full of potholes. Not exactly the best way to get where you're going!

Here, Feng Shui[1] pops up- where we'll transform your environment from a focus obstacle course into your personal productivity sanctuary. And before you raise an eyebrow at the term "Feng Shui," thinking we're about to get all mystical with crystal placements and energy alignments, let me stop you right there. While those ancient Chinese masters were definitely onto something with their understanding of how spaces affect people, we're going to blend their wisdom with modern science to create something really practical for your focus to thrive.

Still hard to believe? Think about it - have you ever noticed how some spaces just make your brain go "Ahhh, now I can think!" while others make your thoughts bounce around like a caffeinated squirrel in a nut factory? That's not random, and it's definitely not just in your head. Just like those ancient Feng Shui practitioners arranged spaces to optimize energy flow, we're going to arrange your environment to optimize your attention flow.

To have a glimpse on how this could look like, close your eyes and picture yourself waltzing into your workspace, and everything's just chef's kiss perfect. Your desk is tidier than Marie Kondo's[2] sock drawer, your chair feels like it was molded for your behind, and the lighting hits your work area just perfectly. Now open your eyes, and don't get frustrated because in this chapter we're about to make it your reality.

Distraction-proof zone

Our brains usually run a sophisticated surveillance operation every single moment. Right now, as you're reading this, it's processing thousands of

---

1. Feng Shui (pronounced "fung shway") is an ancient Chinese practice of arranging spaces to promote wellbeing and optimal functioning. While traditional practitioners focus on energy flow, its core principle - that our environment profoundly impacts our performance - aligns with modern research in environmental psychology and workplace design

2. The Mary Poppins of tidying up and author of "The Life-Changing Magic of Tidying Up." Known as the queen of decluttering, she revolutionized organization with her KonMari Method™. Her approach has become so influential that her name is synonymous with clutter-free living - if your mess had a nemesis, it would be Marie Kondo!

environmental signals – from the brightness of your screen to that pile of papers in your peripheral vision quietly begging you to deal with - even that slight hum from your computer fan is being registered and processed. Now, modern studies have been reporting what those ancient Feng Shui masters somehow knew intuitively - your environment isn't just a passive backdrop to your mental performance, it's an active player in the concentration game. Several reports pointed out the profound effect our work places have on our focus. Therefore, applying a little Feng Shui magic to your workspace isn't all about making it "Instagram-able" - though that's a cool bonus! It's about transforming your area into a focus-boosting spot. An area that doesn't just look neat but actually helps your brain kick into the right gear.

In this chapter, we'll cover it all, from your desk – the center stage of productivity – to the seemingly small often-overlooked elements - like lighting and temperature. But, we're not stopping at the basics. We'll tackle some surprising factors that can transform your space from meh to motivating. Let's roll up our sleeves and get to work!

Visual Zen

We start with the first thing you perceive when you enter a place. How your environment is arranged physically. Everything in your visual field is going to have a say in making or breaking your focus. And just like a photographer wouldn't try to shoot a masterpiece in a cluttered studio, your brain struggles to produce its best work in a chaotic environment.

Your desk is probably your immediate work environment - ground zero for your daily focus battles. Think of it as a launching pad for all your work and ideas. And if rockets need a clear launchpad for takeoff, your thoughts will need a clean space to take flight. When it's tidy and well-organized, it directly influences your ability to concentrate and get things done efficiently.

Research reveals something fascinating about this: when your visual environment is cluttered, multiple objects compete for your neural attention, essentially forcing your brain to work overtime just to filter out unnecessary information. It's like trying to have a conversation in a room where everyone is shouting - technically possible, but exhaustingly inefficient! That pile of papers you've been planning to sort "someday" isn't just taking up physical space; it's actively draining your mental energy.

The evidence for this is compelling: researchers found that people working in organized spaces could focus for longer before feeling distracted. Think of a clutter-free workstation as having the best possible soil for your focus and productivity to sprout. So, without further ado, let's explore some ways to make your workstation more conducive to productivity by making it more simple, practical, and pleasing to the eye...

Tidy and Minimalist

Studies found that people working in cluttered environments show higher levels of cortisol, the stress hormone. So, your messy desk isn't just an eyesore - it's actually stressing you out! The idea behind a minimalist workspace is beautifully simple: **less visual chaos** = **more mental clarity**. If your desk is a stage where every item on it is performing for your attention, then the fewer performers you have, the easier it is to focus on the important ones, right? It's more than just a design trend; it's a powerful tool to enhance focus by eliminating visual distractions.

Getting rid of clutter doesn't mean creating an empty desk; rather, it requires thoughtful curation. Ask yourself: Has this item earned its place on your desk, or is it just there to collect dust and steal your attention? A well-organized desk might include just your computer, a notebook, a pen, and maybe a small plant for a touch of nature.[3] There's nothing else competing for your attention—no paper piles, no scattered supplies—just a clean, calm space that invites focus.

When creating your minimalist workspace, remember that simplicity is the ultimate sophistication. Keep only your daily essentials within arm's reach, tucking occasional-use items neatly into drawers where they won't compete for your attention. Always prioritize quality over quantity in your workspace tools, and maintain clear sight lines across your desk to reduce visual noise that can fragment your focus. One particularly effective strategy is what I call the 'clean sweep' technique – dedicating just five minutes at the end of each day to return everything to its designated home. This small daily habit does more than maintain order; it offers your tomorrow-self a fresh start every morning, providing a clean canvas ready for your best work. Think of it as giving yourself a daily gift of clarity and calm, setting the stage for focused, productive work before the day even begins.

Good old pen and paper

In our world of endless apps and digital tools, there's something almost rebellious about using pen and paper. But this isn't just about nostalgia - research shows that writing by hand activates more regions of the brain than typing does. With a notebook, no battery life to care about, no update required - just pure, distilled thoughts to capture in a judgement-free manner with no formatting is needed. Besides, it has been shown that the physical act of writing things down improves memory retention and helps process information in ways that typing simply can't match. Every time

3. Research shows that having plants in your workspace isn't just aesthetically pleasing – it can significantly boost your cognitive performance. Plants have been shown to increase productivity, enhance attention, reduce mental fatigue, and lower stress levels. Even a single small plant can improve air quality and create a more mentally refreshing environment, making it easier to maintain focus during long work sessions.

you scribble something down, you're giving your brain a mini-workout – not only a finger exercise - while staying fully engaged in the moment.

A well-crafted notebook and reliable pen become more than just writing tools—they're extensions of your brain, helping you outsource ideas and free up mental space. Therefore, invest in tools that feel good to use. Research shows that enjoyable writing tools increased writing frequency noticeably. This doesn't mean you need an expensive fountain pen - just find something that makes you want to write! When you enjoy using your tools, you're more likely to stick with them consistently.

Sorting out the Spaghetti Monster

Next is resolving that tangled mess of cables that looks like it might have eaten a charging cord or two. Research shows that visual disorder – like those chaotic cables from your laptops, monitors, and chargers - can increase cognitive load and get you frustrated quickly. The good news? Implementing a cable management solution will instantly tame these fighting cables - a crucial step in creating a focus-friendly workspace

Start with simple tools like cable clips and sleeves to bundle wires together, and install under-desk trays to hide them from view. For better organization, create a quick 'cable map' as a reference guide, and use color-coding or labels for instant identification – blue for laptop, green for phone charger, red for monitor power. This simple act of tucking away your cables does more than improve appearances – it creates a streamlined, functional workspace where you can focus without visual distraction. You'll be amazed at how much calmer and more focused you feel when you're not staring at a tangle of wires.

Clear Space, Clear Mind

Creating your visual Zen isn't just about aesthetics – it's about engineering an environment that supports and enhances your focus. By thoughtfully curating your workspace, from maintaining a minimalist desk to managing cables and choosing the right tools, you're eliminating unnecessary cognitive load and creating mental space for focus-demanding work. Think of it as preparing a stage for peak performance: when every item has its purpose and place, when visual chaos is replaced with intentional order, your mind is free to focus on what truly matters. Always keep in mind that your physical environment affects your mental performance. The time invested in organizing your space isn't just about tidiness – it's an investment in your daily cognitive performance and productivity. A clear space creates a clear mind, setting the foundation for your best work to emerge.

Furniture Ergonomics

Now that we've decluttered your desk and tamed those wild cables, let's address something equally crucial but often overlooked - how you actually sit at that neatly organized desk. Even the most minimalist workspace won't help if you're constantly squirming in discomfort or wrestling with a chair that seems designed by someone who's never met a human spine. Think about it for a moment: when your back is aching or your neck is stiff, your brain becomes too busy processing those distress signals to focus on anything else.

Studies show that physical discomfort directly impacts cognitive performance, whereas proper ergonomics can transform your workspace from a silent source of distraction into a productivity partner. Research in applied ergonomics have reported that simple interventions don't just reduce physical discomfort – they significantly improve concentration and mental acuity. The Occupational Safety and Health Administration (OSHA) confirms this, saying that well-designed ergonomic furniture can boost productivity substantially. Because when you're not constantly fidgeting to find a comfortable position, your mind is free to focus on the task at hand.

Let's talk about the essential elements that make up this ergonomic foundation for focus.

Active Sitting

Since sitting has been dubbed 'the new smoking,' let's explore how active sitting can transform your workday. Think of active (or dynamic) sitting as a way to keep your body engaged rather than frozen in one position. Unlike traditional static sitting, it allows natural movement while seated, reducing sustained pressure on any single area of your body while keeping your muscles engaged. Research shows this can not only reduce discomfort but also significantly increase how long you can stay focused.

Your active sitting options fall into three main categories: First, ergonomic office chairs - not your typical rocking chair or recliner, but sophisticated seats with adjustable height, lumbar support, and armrests tailored to support proper spine alignment. Next are innovative seating solutions, like cross-legged or meditation-friendly designs[4] , which cater to diverse sitting preferences and encourage natural movement patterns. Finally, stability balls offer another dynamic option, engaging your core and promoting better posture while keeping you alert.

Ideally, you'd create a seating variety system by mixing these options throughout your day. Switch between an ergonomic chair, stability ball, and standing position. This diversity will ensure your physical comfort while maintaining mental engagement. Consider adding an under-desk walking treadmill or pedals to incorporate even more movement into your day. Finally, the best chair is the one that makes you forget you're sitting - if you're constantly thinking about your discomfort, it's probably not the right solution for you.

Sit-Stand Desks

Feeling stuck on a problem? The solution might be as simple as standing up! While many view sit-stand desks as trendy office accessories, research

4. I personally have been using one of those for couple of years now, and it has been a real game changer for me.

reveals they're powerful tools for enhancing how we think and work. Research explains that these desks improve cognitive performance by increasing blood circulation and oxygen flow to the brain.

The evidence is compelling. For example, the "Take-a-Stand" project demonstrated that participants using sit-stand desks reported significant improvements in workplace focus, with 71% feeling more focused and 66% reporting increased productivity. Even more impressive, the Stand More AT Work (SMArT Work) study found that after a year of using sit-stand desks, participants experienced not only a substantial reduction in musculoskeletal problems but also significant improvements in concentration and cognitive function.[5]

The ability to switch between sitting and standing throughout the day isn't just good for your body—it's a powerful tool for maintaining mental alertness. When you feel your attention wandering, simply change positions. This physical shift can help reboot your focus, making complex tasks feel more manageable. After all, when you feel better physically, you're better equipped to maintain concentration and tackle challenging work.

Proper Positioning

Think of positioning as the secret sauce of ergonomics - it costs nothing but can make or break your focus game. Even the most expensive ergonomic chair won't help if you're using it incorrectly. Your body alignment works like a precision machine - when all parts are properly positioned, everything runs smoothly. One misaligned component, and suddenly your brain switches to worrying about physical discomfort instead of focusing on what really matters – getting things done.

---

5. While these studies rely on participants' self-reported improvements, the consistency and magnitude of perceived benefits across different research projects is noteworthy. Even if subjective, a significant reduction in physical discomfort and improved sense of focus represent meaningful changes in people's daily work experience. At the end of the day, how we feel - both physically and mentally - directly impacts our ability to concentrate and perform at our best.

Start with your 'Screen Sweet Spot.' Position your monitor's top at or slightly below eye level, about an arm's length away, with a slight downward tilt. Here's a simple test: if you can high-five your screen, it's probably at the right distance. For multiple monitors, keep your primary screen centered directly in front, with secondary screens angled slightly inward at the same height and distance to minimize head turning.

Your 'Input Zone' - keyboard and mouse - should be positioned so your elbows rest at 90-110 degrees, with wrists floating or lightly supported – never bent. For sitting posture, think '90-90-90': roughly 90-degree angles at your elbows, hips, and knees, with feet flat on the floor or on a footrest, back against the chair using that lumbar support, and shoulders relaxed (not hunched). Combat eye strain with the 20-20-20 rule: every 20 minutes, look at something 20 feet away for 20 seconds. This will provide a mini-vacation for your eyes that can significantly reduce strain.

It's important to remember that the best position is your next position. Keep this as a reminder to include regular movements throughout your day, from micro-adjustments every 15 minutes to stand-sit transitions every 30-45 minutes. Set up your workspace like a pilot's cockpit, with everything within easy reach and optimally positioned to minimize strain.

Investing in Your Cognitive Capital

Consider ergonomic furniture as an investment in your cognitive real estate. While quality ergonomic solutions might cost more upfront, they create an environment where your body and brain can work together optimally. After all, the ability to think clearly and work effectively is priceless.

Environmental Factors

Now that we've optimized your immediate workspace and ergonomics, let's zoom out to consider your broader environment you work in. Ever noticed how you feel razor-sharp in some places but fuzzy-headed in others? The secret to that lies in your environment.

Addressing your surrounding isn't only about comfort; it's more about its impact on your cognitive function, and overall wellbeing. Environmental research has identified a condition called Sick Building Syndrome (SBS), where poor environmental conditions in buildings lead to a range of symptoms including headaches, fatigue, and difficulty concentrating. Studies show that people working in buildings with poor environmental quality can experience a serious decline in cognitive functioning. The culprits? Usually a combination of inadequate ventilation, poor lighting, inconsistent temperature control, and excessive noise.

In this section, we'll discuss some of these environmental factors that play a crucial role in how well your brain functions throughout the day. Getting them right will fend off any discomfort, while actively supporting your cognitive performance.

Lighting

Our brains – like a sophisticated houseplant - need the right kind of light to thrive. Research consistently shows that proper lighting doesn't just help us see better; it fundamentally affects our cognitive performance, attention span, and mental energy. Studies in neuroscience reveal that light directly influences our brain's alertness centers, regulating everything from our focus to our mood. Yet unlike a succulent that simply needs sunlight to flourish, our brains have more specific lighting requirements for optimal performance.

Natural Light: Your Brain's Best Friend

That energized feeling you get from stepping into sunlight is not just good vibes. A study revealed something fascinating: office workers with more natural light exposure don't just perform better at work; they also sleep 46 minutes longer at night. Workers with windows receive 173% more white light exposure during work hours, leading to improved cognitive performance and overall quality of life. All of these perks just by sitting near a window! This research makes a compelling case for prioritizing natural daylight in workspace design - think of it as a two-for-one deal where architectural choices become a wellness program.

Artificial Light: Making the Best of Indoor Life

Since we can't all work in glass houses – though it would be fun, let's explore how to optimize artificial lighting for peak cognitive performance. Research shows different lighting types have distinct impacts on our focus and wellbeing.

Fluorescent lights - the common office villain, can trigger headaches and fatigue. Whereas, *blue light* from screens acts like caffeine for your eyes - beneficial during the day but disruptive when you're winding down. The *full-spectrum bulbs* could offer the next best option to bottling sunshine. They mimic natural light and can trick your brain into thinking you're outdoors - with studies showing they improve alertness, thinking, and overall mood compared to standard fluorescent lighting.

The most advanced option, though, is the *dynamic LED system*. It's a smart lighting solution which mimics natural daylight progression by adjusting color temperature and intensity throughout the day - cooler blue tones in the morning shifting to warmer evening tones. Research shows this system can significantly improve visual comfort, boost alertness and cognitive performance, particularly during afternoon slump periods.

Stuck in a windowless cubicle with standard lighting? Try these focus-saving strategies: Take regular 'light breaks' by stepping outside or near windows during task breaks, invest in a full-spectrum desk lamp for your immediate workspace, and adjust your screen's color temperature using apps like f.lux.[6]

'Light is the most important environmental input, after food and water, in controlling bodily functions.'[7] This quote captures the critical role that light plays in our physiological and cognitive functions – making the brain function as a sophisticated solar panel - feed it the right light, and watch your productivity shine.

Sound

Think silence is always golden for focus? Not quite. While a noisy environment can jeopardize your focus, research shows that the right kind of sound can actually enhance your concentration. It's all about finding your acoustic sweet spot.

According to the World Health Organization (WHO), optimal background noise for focus-demanding work should hover between 35-45 decibels - think quiet library levels. But here's where it gets interesting: moderate ambient noise (around 70 decibels, like coffee shop chatter) can boost creative thinking and problem-solving skills. However, push the noise levels higher, and your brain goes into panic mode, making reading comprehension and information retention nearly impossible.

So how do you create your ideal sound environment in today's open-plan offices? Here are some proven strategies: First, invest in noise-canceling headphones - they're like a forcefield for your focus, blocking out distracting conversations and ambient noise. Next, customize your audio environment– instead of being forced to listen to the surrounding noise.

---

6. A free software that automatically adjusts your screen's color temperature based on the time of day. During daylight hours, it maintains a bright, blue-rich display that matches natural sunlight. As evening approaches, it gradually shifts to warmer, amber tones that reduce blue light exposure - similar to how natural light changes from day to night. This helps reduce eye strain and supports your body's natural sleep-wake cycle.

7. From "The Effects of Light on the Human Body" by Richard Wurtman.

Get creative selecting what your ears listen to and match it to your task. For example, nature sounds for sustained focus (proven to enhance cognitive function), white noise for complex tasks, ambient music for creative work, or complete silence for precision tasks. Finally, if possible, locate or create quiet zones to have uninterrupted focus-intensive work sessions. Many offices now offer designated quiet areas. No quiet zone? Time to channel your inner explorer and find that perfect, secluded spot. Your local library might just become your new best friend.

The bottom line here is not about achieving perfect silence; it's about creating the right acoustic environment for your brain to thrive. Whether you're analyzing data or brainstorming ideas, your soundscape should support your cognitive needs. After all, trying to do brain-intensive work in a noisy environment is technically possible, but definitely not optimal!

Temperature

Just as your computer needs the right operating temperature, your brain has its own thermal sweet spot to function at its best. Research has identified a 'Goldilocks zone'[8] where our cognitive abilities thrive - not too hot, not too cold, but just right.

Studies show that the optimal temperature range for mental performance lies between 71-77°F (22-25°C). Within this range, workers make significantly fewer errors and maintain better focus. Venture outside these boundaries, and your brain's performance suffers: temperatures above 77°F lead to mental fatigue and impaired decision-making, while below 68°F increases error rates and reduces productivity.

Can't control the office thermostat? Try these personal temperature management strategies: Keep a light sweater handy for cold spells, use

8. Referring to the Goldilocks principle – named after the famous fairy tale "The Goldilocks and the three bears"- which focuses on the amount and type to be "just right" to maximize effectiveness (i.e. not too little and not too much)!

a small desk fan when it's warm, and avoid sitting directly under HVAC[9] vents where temperature fluctuates most. Layer your clothing for flexibility, and consider a USB-powered heating pad or cooling fan for precise personal comfort and to be with you on the go. One more factor not to overlook is humidity - maintaining levels between 40-60% can significantly impact how comfortable you feel at any temperature.

Purposeful Workspaces: Think Zones

One final thing you should always keep in mind - different types of work demand certain environments to perform at your best. Just as you wouldn't try to nap in your kitchen, or cook dinner in your bedroom (college days aside), your brain performs best when spaces are specifically designed for their intended cognitive functions. In other words, match your space with the task you're handling. For example, focus-demanding work requires quiet, distraction-free zones with sound control and visual barriers, whereas collaborative work thrives in movement-friendly spaces that encourage interaction.

Even with limited space, you can still create effective work zones by adapting your environment throughout the day - it just requires a bit more creativity. Think of it like a tiny house where one room transforms throughout the day to serve different purposes. Here's how to make it work: Use time blocks to schedule different activities for different times (morning for focus-demanding work, afternoon for collaboration); adjust your environment with lighting (bright for focus, dim for creative work) and sound levels to signal different modes to your brain (quiet for concentration, background noise for casual tasks); and create temporary boundaries using movable dividers or headphones when needed.

Finally, whether you have an entire office or just a corner desk, the key is your consistency in creating clear boundaries between different types of work. When you regularly pair certain environmental cues with specific

---

9. Heating, Ventilation, and Air Conditioning.

types of work, your brain learns these associations, making it easier to switch between different work modes even in the same physical space.

Environmental Mastery

To wrap up, studies show that optimizing light, sound, and temperature together does not just add up their individual benefits – it's multiplying them. Now, if we think of your brain as a professional athlete and your environment is its training facility, then using the right conditions in this facility will make your brain reach new heights.

The magic happens when you orchestrate all the elements together. For peak morning performance, combine bright, cool lighting with library-quiet sound levels and slightly cooler temperatures. Shift to moderate, warm lighting with gentle background noise and slightly warmer temperatures for afternoon creative sessions. And when working with limited environmental control, create a personal focus bubble using task lighting, noise-canceling technology, and portable temperature solutions.

From Physical to Digital: Your Second Workspace

In today's world, half of your focus battles happen on your screens. Think about it: how many times have you sat down at your beautifully arranged desk, only to open your laptop and face an avalanche of random files, countless tabs, and endless notifications? Research shows that digital clutter significantly increases cognitive load, with the average worker losing hours every week to digital distractions. Your digital space needs just as much intentional design as your physical one - maybe even more. After all, no physical desk ever sent you push notifications about your friend's cat photos!

Your digital focus transformation starts with **screen organization**. Every pixel on your screen should earn its place. Create distinct digital desktops, each optimized for specific types of work: a *Focus-intensive Work Zone* with minimal icons and core work apps, a *Communication Hub* for email and messaging, a *Research Station* for browsers and reference materials, and a *Creative Space* for design tools and inspiration. This organized approach creates clear boundaries between different types of work and helps maintain focus by keeping distractions at bay.

App management is equally crucial - think of your apps like tools in a seasoned craftsperson's workshop. You want the best ones, in the right places, ready when needed. But having too many tools can be just as problematic as having too few, with research showing that the average professional loses up to thirty minutes per day just switching between applications. So, select apps that solve specific problems, integrate well with other tools, don't duplicate existing functions, and genuinely save more time than they take to use. Also, a great thing to do is to review your app ecosystem quarterly. If you haven't used an app in three months, it probably doesn't deserve space in your digital workspace.

Finally, to have the upper hand when it comes to **notification** - think of them as guests at an exclusive club. Not everyone deserves VIP access to your attention. The average professional gets interrupted by notifications many times per day costing up to 2 hours lost to divided attention and refocusing. Therefore, it's indispensable to create a strict priority system: something like the 'Double Filter' rule - a notification must be both urgent AND important (critical messages, key deadlines) to interrupt your focus time. Everything else can wait for your next scheduled check-in to batch process (important but not urgent matter).

Remember: Your attention is the most valuable currency in today's digital economy. Just as you wouldn't let your physical desk become cluttered with distractions, don't let your digital workspace become a source of constant interruption. By thoughtfully organizing your digital environment, managing your apps, and controlling notifications, you create a second workspace that supports rather than sabotages your focus.

Putting It All Together

Just as a Formula 1 car needs the perfect track to demonstrate its true potential, your focus machine requires an optimized environment to perform at its peak. Throughout this chapter, we've designed that perfect track, transforming your workspace from a focus obstacle course into a productivity sanctuary.

From Visual Zen to ergonomics, from environmental conditions to digital spaces, we've engineered every aspect of your environment to work in harmony:

- *Physical Space*: A decluttered, body-friendly foundation.
- *Environmental Conditions:* Your personalized light, sound, and temperature.
- *Digital Domain*: A distraction-free screen environment.

Remember: your environment isn't just a backdrop – it's an active participant in your cognitive performance. When these elements work together, they create a sophisticated focus ecosystem where sustained attention becomes your natural state rather than a constant struggle.

Connecting the Dots

Your Complete Focus System

We began our journey by building a powerful focus engine, assembling it piece by piece - from clear goals as our GPS to habits as our automatic transmission. But we quickly learned that a high-performance vehicle needs more than just an engine. This engine needs comprehensive support through strategic nutrition, quality sleep, and regular movement. We, also, learned that our physical foundation acts as the chassis, while mental resilience serves as our operating system, helping us navigate challenging conditions.

Finally, we explored how even the best-equipped vehicle needs the right track conditions to perform at its peak. We've seen how to optimize our environment - from decluttering our physical space to managing our digital landscape - creating ideal conditions for sustained focus.

Together, these elements form a complete high-performance focus system:

- **The Engine**: Your core focus skills and habits.
- **The Vehicle**: Your body and mind working in harmony.
- **The Track**: Your optimized environment, both physical and digital.

What we've created isn't just a collection of techniques - it's a comprehensive focus ecosystem designed to transform sustained attention from a constant struggle into your natural state. Each component supports and enhances the others, creating a powerful upward spiral of improvement.

The blueprint is complete. The components are optimized. The track is prepared. Your focus machine isn't just stronger - it's systematically optimized for peak performance. Now it's time to take this machine out for a spin and show the world what it can do.

PART IV

FOCUS ROADMAP

"Great things are done by a series of small things brought together." -Vincent van Gogh

From Knowledge to Action

Have you ever finished reading a transformative book, felt incredibly inspired, and then found yourself staring at a blank page, unsure where to begin? You're not alone. Looking at all these strategies might feel like standing at the base of Mount Everest wearing flip-flops! It's natural to feel overwhelmed. Research shows that trying to implement too many changes simultaneously often leads to abandoning all efforts within the first month. But here's the fascinating thing about change: it's more like growing your hair than flipping a switch. You might not notice the daily progress, but give it time, and the transformation becomes undeniable.

Think of everything we've covered so far as gathering pieces for a powerful focus toolkit. We've explored the mechanics of attention, discovered what fractures our focus, and learned how to create the right conditions for concentration. Now comes the exciting part – turning these insights into action in a way that works uniquely for you.

In this part, we'll walk through everything you need to build lasting change. You'll discover why creating simple systems works better than relying on motivation alone, and how small, strategic changes can transform your ability to concentrate. Together, we'll map out where you are, identify your best opportunities for improvement, and create a practical roadmap to get there. We'll explain how to track your progress and navigate challenges along the way. Finally, we'll wrap up with the Focus Commandments, timeless principles that will guide you throughout your focus journey.

Systems Advantage: Beyond Goals and Motivation

Ever asked yourself why most New Year's resolutions barely survive past February? It's because they rely on motivation—that initial spark of enthusiasm that inevitably fades. While motivation is great for getting started, it's notoriously unreliable for the long haul. But here's something fascinating: research shows that people who build systems consistently outperform those who focus solely on goals. So, when goals tell you where to go, systems determine how you'll get there—and more importantly, how you'll stay there.

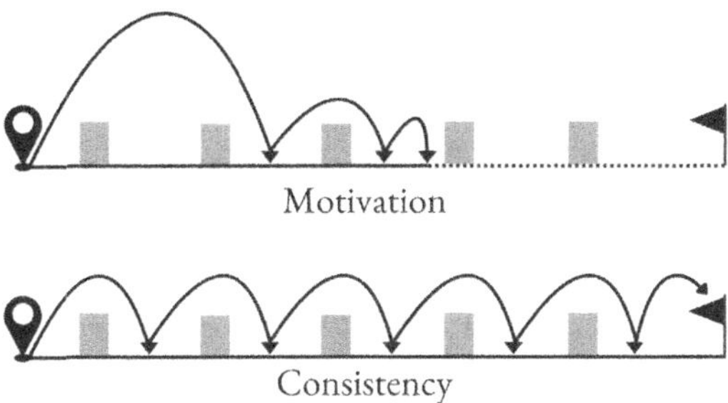

Reaching your goal: Motivation's erratic path versus consistency's steady progress

To create such a system-based approach, you need to understand two key forces: consistency and discipline. Consistency is about showing up regularly, executing actions regardless of how you feel. Discipline, contrary to popular belief, isn't about iron willpower—it emerges naturally from well-designed systems that reduce decision-making friction and create automatic behaviors.

This transformation from goal-focused to system-based thinking happens in two distinct stages. Stage One is like learning to drive—every action requires conscious effort and deliberate execution that feels challenging. You actively think about maintaining focus, following routines, and resisting distractions. Stage Two is where brain plasticity works its magic: like an experienced driver navigating without conscious thought, your focus-supporting behaviors become automatic. Each time you follow your system, you're sculpting mental pathways that make concentration more natural and efficient.

The power of systems lies in their ability to transform extraordinary effort into ordinary routine through strategic automation. Rather than relying on willpower or daily motivation, systems work by reducing two key frictions:

- Decision-making (when and how to focus)
- Environmental setup (where and under what conditions)

This way, the system bypasses emotional resistance entirely—it doesn't matter whether you feel like focusing or not. The decisions are already made, and the environment is already set.

Let's see how this works in practice by comparing two approaches:

Goal-Based Thinking: "I need to focus better today, so I should probably find a quiet spot and try to concentrate."

System-Based Thinking: "It's 9 AM—my environment is already set up, my phone is in another room, and this is my dedicated deep work time."

The difference is clear: the goal-based approach requires fresh decision-making each day, depleting your mental energy before you even begin. The system-based approach, however, eliminates these decisions entirely. Your environment and schedule are predetermined, leaving you free to focus on the work itself.

This evolution from conscious effort to automatic execution is the crucial transformation we're after—the tipping point where focus shifts from something you do to something you are. Like a practiced athlete who doesn't think about their form during a game, your trained brain maintains focus without conscious effort, freeing up mental energy for the work itself.

Consider how the Egyptian Nobel laureate Naguib Mahfouz embodied these principles to be able to craft over 400 stories, novels, and screenplays. "Without discipline, nothing can be accomplished," he maintained, and his life proved this maxim. Despite the demands of a full-time civil service job and raising two children, he devised a system of non-negotiable writing hours that never wavered – three hours each evening after his nap, except for weekends, and holidays. After retirement, he shifted to writing daily from 10 AM to 1 PM.

"Waiting for inspiration would only yield a few novels," he observed. "Instead, I gave the muse my office hours!" By treating writing as a professional commitment rather than an artistic whim, he transformed creative work from an unpredictable art into a reliable craft. His consistency in showing up every day, combined with the discipline embedded in his system, made productivity automatic rather than optional. Even on his busiest days, there was no decision to make—writing time was as non-negotiable as his government job.

Remember: it's not about perfection—it's about showing up consistently, especially when you don't feel like it. The ultimate goal is to create a framework so reliable that discipline becomes unnecessary, and focus becomes a natural, almost unconscious state of being. This sets the stage to move on to explore how these systems grow stronger over time through the power of compounding.

The Compounding Effect

Albert Einstein called compound interest "the eighth wonder of the world." While he was referring to finance, this principle applies just as powerfully to focus. Just as money grows through compound interest, your focus systems strengthen through compound improvements, following a simple equation:

Progress = choice × frequency × reinforcement

Where, **choice** is the quality of an action (positive or negative value), **frequency** is how often you take that action, and **reinforcement** is how deeply that action becomes integrated into your mental pathways.

This model explains why true progress isn't linear. Each day you follow your system, you're not just maintaining a routine—you're building upon previous progress, creating exponential rather than linear growth. A 1% improvement, compounded daily over a year, makes you 37 times better than when you started.

Consider this practical example: Start with a 10-minute session of undistracted focus. Adding just six seconds (1% improvement) each day would lead to 47 minutes of focus after a year through simple addition. But when these improvements compound—each day building upon the stronger foundation of the day before—that same tiny daily improvement can lead to 6.3 hours of sustained focus.[1]

Think of it like clearing a path through a dense forest. Simple addition is like cutting the same width each day. Compounding is like having each pass naturally widen the trail, making subsequent journeys progressively easier. Each time you engage your focus system, you're not just maintaining a habit—you're strengthening your mental pathways, making execution increasingly natural and effortless.

This explains why the early days of any system feel challenging but get progressively easier. Remember: your daily choices are the multipliers that determine your direction of growth. Positive choices compound into upward spirals of improvement, while negative choices multiply into downward spirals of limitation. The power of compounding works both ways—choose wisely.

Making Compound Growth Work For You

Now that we understand how compound growth works, let's turn this knowledge into practical action. Instead of aiming for dramatic transformations, focus on tiny, consistent improvements that accumulate

1. While the mathematical model suggests turning 10 minutes into 6 hours of focus time in a year, real-world improvements are typically more modest. Nevertheless, the principle itself remains powerful: small, consistent improvements compound into remarkable transformations.

over time. Like any powerful system, this approach requires scheduled monitoring and long-term thinking.

Track your progress strategically by looking for patterns over time rather than fixating on daily measurements. In the first month, focus on consistency rather than duration—the goal is to make the practice automatic, like brushing your teeth. By day 90, notice how starting your focus sessions becomes easier. At six months, observe how your natural focus duration has increased. After a year, review how your entire relationship with focus has transformed.

Think of your focus system like an investment portfolio. Your initial deposits might seem modest—perhaps just 10 minutes of undistracted work session—but as you consistently reinvest your gains, your returns begin to multiply. This long-term thinking is smarter - it replaces the common "all or nothing" mindset that leads to burnout. It's why systems ultimately triumph over focusing on goals alone. While goals provide direction, systems—especially those built with compound growth in mind—create lasting change through consistent, incremental improvement.

Beyond Growth: The Power of Clear Vision

Understanding how improvements compound is crucial, but before you start building your focus system, you need a clear picture of your starting point and destination. Most people jump straight to imagining their success—picturing the finish line without considering the hurdles along the track. Research shows that positive thinking – visualizing the desired outcome, while temporarily motivating, often falls short of producing real results. However, mental contrasting – a more balanced approach – proves to be far more effective.

Mental contrasting helps us see the complete picture—both where we want to go and what stands in our way. I learned this lesson firsthand while writing this book. Simply thinking positively about completing the book wasn't enough. The project gained real momentum only after I printed the cover and displayed it on my wall, alongside a list of obstacles I needed to overcome. This combination—the visual reminder of my goal and the clear understanding of challenges ahead—transformed vague aspirations into concrete steps I needed to take to achieve my goal. The proof? You're reading this book now!

This approach aligns with research findings that show people who write down their goals are 40% more likely to achieve them than those who don't. But the real power comes from combining written goals with a clear view of potential obstacles.

SCAN Your Focus Landscape

Before rushing to implement any changes, take time to thoroughly map your focus terrain. Think of it like using Google Earth—you start with a broad view from orbit, then gradually zoom in to street level. This perspective allows you to see both the full landscape and crucial details that might be missed by looking only at ground level.

Mapping your focus ecosystem will assess where you stand. Let's see how this works through a practical example. Imagine you're a researcher working in an open-plan lab with a crucial grant proposal deadline approaching. Here's how you'd **SCAN** your situation:

Strengths: You notice you produce your best writing early in the morning before the lab gets busy, and you can maintain deep focus for extended periods once you get into a flow state. These aren't just habits—they're valuable clues about when and how you work best.

Challenges: The open-plan lab environment means constant interruptions from colleagues, equipment noise, and impromptu discussions. Grant writing requires sustained concentration that's difficult to maintain with these disruptions. Instead of ignoring these obstacles, acknowledge them as part of your planning.

Assets: You have access to a quiet meeting room that's usually empty before 9 AM, noise-canceling headphones, and supportive colleagues who understand the importance of grant deadlines. Your institution's library also offers private study rooms. These existing resources could be key elements of your focus strategy.

Needs: You might need a system for managing colleague interruptions, a clear signal when you're in focus-intensive work mode, and perhaps a better way to organize your grant-writing materials for quick setup and teardown in different spaces.

With your SCAN complete, you can now identify leverage points where small changes will create the biggest impact. For the grant proposal example, three key areas emerge:

Morning Routine - *First Domino Piece*: Starting early transforms the challenge entirely. Arriving at the lab by 7 AM provides two hours of pristine focus time before colleagues arrive. This isn't just about having a quiet space—it's about setting up a domino effect of productivity. Those first two hours of undistracted work create momentum that carries through the entire day. Even when the lab gets busy later, you've already accomplished your most focus-demanding work.

Environment Setup: Instead of fighting the open-plan layout, design your environment strategically. Set up camp in the quiet meeting room during your morning sessions. Create a clear "do not disturb" signal using your noise-canceling headphones. Keep your grant-writing materials organized in a portable system so you can quickly establish your focus space anywhere.

Recovery: Grant writing demands intense mental effort. Plan needed breaks between writing sessions—perhaps a short walk outside or a few minutes of stretching. Schedule your most challenging writing tasks when your energy is highest, using the natural dips in your day for less demanding tasks like organizing references or formatting. Your ability to maintain focus throughout the writing process depends heavily on how well you recover between sessions.

Finding Your Leverage Points

With all these potential areas for improvement, you might be wondering: where should you begin? The **Impact-Effort Matrix**—similar to the Eisenhower Matrix we used for task prioritization—can help you identify your most effective starting points.

The Impact-Effort Matrix is a simple but powerful compass for change. Just as a smart investor looks for the best return on investment, this tool helps you identify which focus improvements will give you the biggest results for your effort. By evaluating each potential change based on its impact (how much it helps) and effort (how hard it is to implement), you can make strategic choices about where to start your focus transformation.

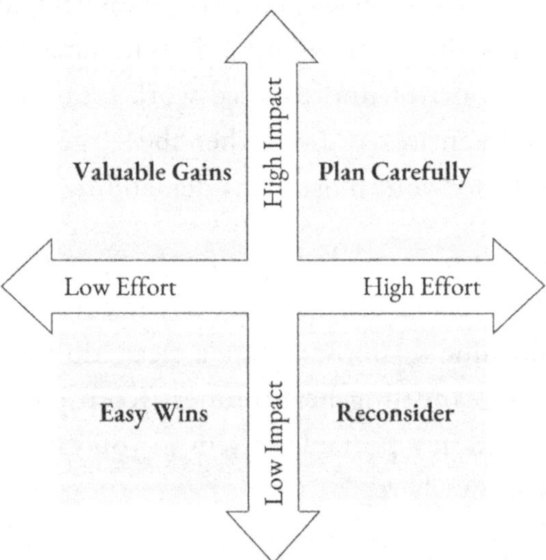

The Impact-Effort Matrix: A strategic tool for prioritizing focus improvements based on their potential impact and required effort

The Impact-Effort Matrix breaks down potential changes into four categories:

High Impact/Low Effort = **Valuable Gains**

These are your prime leverage points—changes that give you the biggest return for minimal investment. For example:

- Moving your phone to another room during focus time.
- Setting up your workspace the night before.

High Impact/High Effort = **Plan Carefully**

These changes matter significantly but require more resources and preparation. Schedule these for later phases after you've built momentum through easier wins. Research shows that successfully completing smaller challenges first builds your belief in your ability to change—what psychologists call "self-efficacy.[2]" This confidence becomes crucial fuel for tackling bigger challenges later.

Low Impact/Low Effort = **Easy Wins**

While not game-changers on their own, these small, and modest victories help build momentum and confidence in your system. Each success, no matter how small, reinforces your belief in your ability to change, creating a positive feedback loop of motivation and achievement.

Low Impact/High Effort = **Reconsider**

These changes rarely justify the resources they require. Best to avoid or find alternative approaches that offer better returns on your investment of time and energy.

---

2. Research shows that when we're struggling with a task, we often have low confidence in our ability to succeed (low self-efficacy). Starting with manageable wins helps build this essential confidence, making us more likely to tackle and persist with bigger challenges.

Using Your Matrix: Implementation Steps

To put the Impact-Effort Matrix into action, you need to begin with high-impact, low-effort changes to be more likely to maintain your improvement efforts long-term, Here's how:

Start with Power Moves – *High Impact/Low Effort*

Begin with these foundation-setting changes:

- Create a distraction-free morning routine (no phone for first hour).

- Designate non-negotiable blocks for focus-demanding work.

Build Momentum - *Low Impact/Low Effort*

After establishing your foundations, reinforce them with easy wins:

- Use a basic timer for focus sessions (simple 25-minute countdowns).

- Create a simple task prioritization system (daily top-three tasks list).

- Establish clear workspace boundaries (designated focus zones, "do not disturb" signals).

These small wins prove to yourself that change is possible, creating positive momentum for more challenging improvements which feel less daunting.

Tackle Bigger Challenges - *High Impact/High Effort*

With momentum established, take on more substantial changes:

- Developing a comprehensive focus protocol.

- Restructuring your digital environment.

- Build advanced recovery systems.

These changes require more effort but build upon your earlier successes.

Avoid Resource Drains - *Low Impact/High Effort*

Skip these tempting but inefficient changes:

- Complex productivity apps requiring extensive setup.
- Elaborate scheduling systems.
- Over-engineered workspace modifications.

These might seem impressive but rarely justify their setup and maintenance costs.

This isn't about implementing everything at once. When building a house—you need a solid foundation before adding walls and a roof. Each successful change supports the next, creating a structure that stands the test of time.

Your Focus Launch Framework

Having already written down your goals and identified potential obstacles, it's time to turn this knowledge into action. Just as a rocket launch follows a carefully planned sequence, transforming your focus requires a strategic timeline. While you might have heard of the 21-day rule for habit formation, modern research shows habits can actually take anywhere from 18 to 254 days to form.[3] That's why we'll focus on a 90-day launch sequence—long enough to see real results and establish patterns, yet not so long that you lose momentum or tracking becomes unwieldy.

Consider keeping your 90-day plan visible in your workspace—this visual reminder will help maintain your accountability throughout the journey.

---

3. The popular 21-day rule originated from Dr. Maxwell Maltz's 1960 observations as a plastic surgeon, when he noticed patients took about 21 days to adjust to their new physical changes. While this became widely cited as the standard time for habit formation, modern research shows the process is far more variable, making our 90-day framework a more realistic timeline for establishing sustainable focus habits.

This timeline provides a structured yet flexible framework to build and strengthen your focus system systematically.

The First 30 Days - Foundation Building

Your first month focuses on establishing core habits that create immediate wins. Instead of trying to change everything at once, you'll concentrate on high-impact, low-effort changes that build confidence and momentum.

Begin *Week One* by implementing key morning habits. Choose a specific wake-up time, create a phone-free morning routine, and prepare your workspace the night before. These fundamental changes set the tone for your entire day and require minimal effort to maintain.

In *Week Two*, establish basic environmental controls. Designate your primary focus spaces, remove common distractions, and create clear "do not disturb" signals. Just as importantly, communicate these new boundaries to people usually around when you're working - this creates social support for your focus practice.

Week Three introduces structured focus blocks. Start small with 25-minute sessions during your peak energy times. Don't worry about duration at this stage; focus instead on establishing the habit of dedicated work periods. This builds the foundation for longer sessions later.

Finally, *Week Four* develops simple recovery protocols. Create clear start and end rituals for your work blocks, and plan strategic breaks between sessions. These boundaries help your brain distinguish between focus time and rest time, making both more effective.

Remember, this first month isn't about perfection - it's about establishing basic habits that will support more advanced practices later. Keep changes small and achievable, celebrating each successful implementation as a win for your focus system.

Your Second Month – System Refinement

While your first month focused on implementing tiny changes and collecting easy wins without the pressure of tracking, your second month is about becoming more systematic. With your foundation in place, it's time to optimize what's working and introduce more structure to your practice.

Fine-tune your routines based on what you've learned: adjust the timing of your focus blocks, modify break durations, and refine your environment setup. Now that these basics feel more natural, you can start gradually extending your focus sessions and developing stronger boundaries.

This is also when you'll introduce tracking into your practice. Begin monitoring your progress with basic systems and markers—not to add pressure, but to understand what's working best for you. These measurements will help you strengthen the habits you've built and make informed adjustments to your system.

The progression is natural: first establish the habits with minimal pressure, then systematically reinforce and improve them through careful observation and adjustment.

Your Final Month – Integration and Expansion

By your third month, you've established consistent habits and tracking systems. Now it's time to weave these separate elements into one cohesive system and prepare for long-term sustainability.

Start implementing more demanding changes. Create contingency plans for challenging days (like backup focus spots when your usual space is unavailable), and build accountability systems (such as sharing your focus goals with colleagues or scheduling regular progress reviews). This is also when you can begin extending your focus sessions even further and enhancing your recovery practices, building upon the foundation you've established.

Work on making your recovery practices more robust and systematic. Move beyond basic breaks to implement strategic recovery - like scheduling energizing activities between focus blocks, using specific techniques for mental reset (breathing exercises, brief meditation), and matching recovery duration to work intensity.

Create seamless transitions between different parts of your system to protect against unintentional distractions. When you link your morning routine directly to your first focus block through a smooth progression (morning exercise → shower → breakfast → focused work), you leave no gaps for distractions to slip in. These automatic sequences become like guardrails for your attention, preventing unconscious drift into time-wasting activities.

Finally, prepare for long-term success by developing maintenance protocols. Create simple checklists for regular system reviews, identify early warning signs that your focus practice needs adjustment, and establish clear criteria for when and how to adapt your system as circumstances change. Think of this as creating your focus system's operating manual—guidelines that will help you maintain and evolve your practice long after these 90 days.

While this timeline provides structure, it should be adapted to your needs. The key isn't rigid adherence to a schedule but steady progress in building your focus system. Like a skilled chef adjusting recipes to available ingredients, modify this timeline to match your circumstances while keeping the core principle: progressive improvement that compounds over time.

Tracking and Troubleshooting

Just as writing down goals significantly increases achievement rates, tracking your progress is crucial for maintaining momentum and identifying areas for improvement. Think of tracking as your focus system's dashboard—it helps you navigate your journey and spot potential issues before they become roadblocks.

Start with *brief daily check-ins*—two-minute pulse checks that keep you aligned with your goals. Ask yourself simple questions: Did you follow your system today? What worked particularly well? Where did you face resistance? These quick assessments help you stay connected to your practice without becoming overwhelmed by data.

Complement these with *weekly reviews*—fifteen-minute sessions dedicated to deeper analysis. Review your daily notes for emerging patterns, assess how your system is performing, and plan adjustments for the coming week. This weekly rhythm helps you catch and address small issues before they become habits.

Set aside thirty minutes each month for *broader evaluations* of your transformation. This is your chance to step back and examine your focus practice as a whole. Track two key areas to ensure your system evolves with your needs:

- ***Measurable Progress***: Monitor quantitative metrics like focus session duration, distraction frequency, and recovery time after interruptions

- ***System Health***: Track qualitative indicators such as ease of starting sessions, work quality, energy levels, and your overall sense of control

As you track your progress, you'll likely encounter common challenges. Understanding these in advance helps you navigate them effectively, for example:

- When your tracking shows inconsistent practice, you might be tempted to blame motivation. Instead of waiting to feel motivated, remember that systems trump willpower. Your focus practice becomes as unpredictable as your mood when you rely on motivation alone. Follow your routines regardless of mood, track consistency rather than intensity, and treat your focus blocks as non-negotiable appointments. Most importantly, build environmental triggers that work even when motivation doesn't.

- Your data might also reveal frequent system breakdowns—a sign you're attempting too much change at once. This "*too-much-too-soon*" trap often leads to no change at all. When this happens, return to your smallest viable action, focus on one change until it becomes automatic, and use the Impact-Effort Matrix to prioritize your next steps. Remember the compound effect—small, consistent changes create lasting transformation.

- Watch out for "*perfectionism paralysis*," where tracking itself becomes a burden. After all, a functioning "good enough" system beats a perfect plan that never starts. Keep your measurements minimal but effective, focus on progress trends rather than perfect scores, and maintain a simple tracking system. Embrace the minimum effective dose, keeping your base system simple and adding complexity only after mastering the basics.

Remember, tracking is a tool to support your focus practice, not an end in itself. It isn't about judgment—it's about gathering intelligence. Each challenge your tracking reveals is valuable data showing where your system needs strengthening. Use this information to refine your approach, remembering that a good system isn't one that never faces challenges, but one that helps you navigate through them effectively.

PART V

FOCUS COMMANDMENTS

"Concentrate all your thoughts upon the work at hand. The sun's rays do not burn until brought to a focus."
-Alexander Graham Bell

Your North Star

Here we arrive at the core teachings that will guide you through any challenge, change, or choice. These aren't just rules; they're the distilled wisdom of everything we've explored together, crystallized into essential principles that stand the test of time and circumstance.

Throughout our journey, certain universal truths have emerged consistently—from understanding attention's foundations to optimizing your environment, from building better habits to maintaining physical and mental wellbeing. The commandments – we discuss here - capture these core insights, adding crucial principles to complete your focus toolkit. They represent both a culmination of our journey and a compass for the path ahead, one you can return to whenever you need to realign your focus practice.

Start Small, Stay Consistent

Principle: Tiny improvements compound into remarkable results.

Why: The path to extraordinary focus isn't paved with dramatic changes but with small, consistent improvements. 1% improvements, compounded daily, lead to remarkable transformations over time. Sustainable progress comes from starting so small you can't fail, then building momentum through consistency. Like a snowball rolling downhill, each small success builds upon the last, creating momentum that grows increasingly powerful.

Action:

- *Begin with minimal viable actions:* 1. Start with ridiculously small focus sessions (even just 10 minutes). 2. Make improvements so tiny they're impossible to fail.

- *Keep sustainable pace:* 1. Focus on consistency over intensity. 2. Celebrate small wins to reinforce the habit. 3. Progress at a rate you can maintain.

- *Keep momentum alive:* 1. Track your progress. 2. Acknowledge improvements. 3. Build on small successes.

Remember: Just as a garden grows through daily tending rather than occasional intense effort, your focus capacity develops through regular, small acts of attention. Each modest step creates a foundation for the next, building a sustainable path to better concentration.

Trust the Process

Principle: Systems trump motivation.

Why: Motivation is temporary; systems are permanent. Research shows that well-designed systems consistently outperform even the strongest willpower. When you build reliable systems, discipline becomes automatic rather than force of will.

Action:

- *Build routines*: 1. Create automatic triggers to get you into focus mode smoothly. 2. Make good choices your default.

- *Focus on process over outcomes*: 1. Measure adherence to the steps you have in your systems (not on outcomes). 2. Trust your routines even when motivation wavers. 3. Let your systems handle decision-making (spare yourself decision fatigue).

- *Maintain and refine:* 1. Regularly evaluate system effectiveness. 2. Adjust based on results. 3. Keep what works, improve what doesn't.

Remember: When you trust the process, discipline becomes less about forcing yourself to focus and more about following established patterns. Your system becomes your strength.

Honor Your Limited Resources

Principle: Your time and mental energy are your most precious, finite resources.

Why: In our hyper-connected world, both time and mental bandwidth are under constant assault. No one will protect these resources for you—it's entirely your responsibility. As Warren Buffett noted, "The difference between successful people and very successful people is that very successful people say no to almost everything." —protecting their non-renewable resource of time. Meanwhile, research shows that our brains have adapted to modern media's constant stimulation—but not necessarily for the better. Digital overconsumption depletes the mental energy needed for focus-demanding work, with studies revealing that many people would rather receive mild electric shocks than sit alone with their thoughts away from their phones - highlighting how dependent we've become on constant digital engagement. The good news? Just as your brain adapted to constant stimulation and distraction, it can be retrained to be focused through intentional practice.

Action:

Practice Digital Minimalism (low-information diet)[1]

- *Create deliberate periods of "digital fasting.":* 1. Start with 30-minute phone-free periods - gradually extend to longer durations. 2. Designate phone-free zones in your home.

- *Choose high-quality mental input:* 1. Read physical books. 2. Engage in single-activity entertainment - sustain focusing on watching something while not scrolling.

- *Train your attention muscle:* 1. Take device-free walks. 2. Practice sustaining single thoughts for some time. 3. Build comfort with mental quiet - embrace periods of boredom as focus training.

Guard Your Time

- Develop clear criteria for what deserves your attention.

- Create protocols for declining distractions gracefully.

- Set and maintain firm boundaries.

- What you don't do is as important as what you do – selective attention requires selective rejection.

- Own your attention - every 'yes' to a distraction is a 'no' to your focus.

Remember: Honoring your limited resources isn't about being difficult—it's about being deliberate. Each moment of intentional digital quietness isn't just an absence of distraction—it's actively rewiring your

---

1. Consciously limiting your consumption of non-essential information (news, social media, endless browsing) to preserve your mental energy for what truly matters.

mental pathways toward better focus. Each 'no' to a distraction is a 'yes' to your focus. Choose wisely what you allow to consume your precious time and mental energy.

Create Before You Consume

Principle: Start your day as a producer, not a consumer.

Why: Building on your protected mental energy and time, this commandment transforms defense into offense. Your mind is sharpest in the morning, making it the perfect time for creation rather than consumption. When you begin your day by creating rather than consuming, you set a powerful precedent for how your protected mental energy will be used.

Action:

- Establish a creation-first morning routine.
- Delay email and social media until after your first creative block.
- Schedule creative work during your peak mental hours.
- Transform your morning from passive consumption to active creation.
- Use your fresh mental energy for your most important work.

Remember: Choose to be a creator before becoming a consumer. Your best mental energy deserves your highest-value activities.

Guard Your Environment

Principle: Your workspace is a sacred ground that shapes your behavior.

Why: Research shows that your environment doesn't just reflect your focus state—it actively creates it. Every element in your space either supports your focus or steals it, making your workspace a key determinant of your concentration ability.

Action:

- *Design your space with intention:* 1. Clear all surfaces of unnecessary items. 2. Position essential tools strategically. 3. Eliminate visual clutter and cable mess.

- *Create dedicated zones:* 1. Designate specific areas for different activities. 2. Establish clear boundaries between work and rest. 3. Maintain distinct spaces for focus-demanding vs. casual work.

- *Treat your workspace as a professional tool:* 1. Maintain its organization daily. 2. Update its setup based on your needs. 3. Protect it from gradual clutter creep.

Remember: Your brain deserves a workspace that supports its best performance. Just as a surgeon needs a sterile operating room and a chef requires a clean kitchen, your focus demands an environment designed for concentration. When you treat your workspace as sacred ground, it becomes a powerful ally in maintaining attention.

Single-Task with Pride

Principle: The power of doing one thing excellently.

Why: As Mozart once observed, "The shorter way to do many things is to only do one thing at a time." When you divide your attention across multiple tasks, you're not being more efficient—you're diluting your focus. Think of your attention as having 10 units: giving all 10 to one task produces excellence, while dividing them among three tasks gives each a mediocre 3/10. What feels like efficiency in multitasking is actually your brain frantically switching contexts, draining your mental energy and compromising quality.

Action:

- Give each task your complete, undivided attention.
- Embrace single-tasking as a mark of professional excellence.
- Remove task-switching triggers from your environment.
- Set clear start and end points for focus-demanding work.
- Take pride in doing one thing excellently.

Remember: Single-tasking isn't a limitation—it's a superpower. It's choosing to do things well rather than simultaneously.

Monitor Your Mental State

Principle: Your mind's condition determines your focus quality.

Why: Even with perfect systems and boundaries in place, your focus fluctuates based on your mental condition. Internal disruptions—like social media comparison, unprocessed emotions, or unaddressed stress—can hijack your attention more effectively than any external distraction. Just as a pilot continuously monitors their instruments, you must stay aware of your mental conditions.

Action:

- Regularly check in with your mental barometer – track mood impacts on focus.
- Notice what enhances or depletes your mental energy.
- Limit exposure to comparative content that breeds frustration.
- Address emotional disturbances before they affect your focus.
- Adjust your focus demands and workload based on your mental capacity.

Remember: Your mind isn't a machine—it's a living system that requires constant monitoring and maintenance. Stay aware of your mental weather patterns, and adjust your focus practice to match your current capacity, ensuring optimal focus conditions.

Respect Recovery

Principle: Rest is not a reward—it's a prerequisite for excellence.

Why: Just as athletes grow stronger during recovery, not during training, your focus capacity builds during strategic rest periods. Recovery isn't what happens after focusing—it's what enables focus in the first place. Your brain, like any high-performance tool, requires regular maintenance to function at its peak.

Action:

- Schedule recovery periods with the same priority as work sessions.
- Build renewal rituals between focus blocks - brief walks, stretching, breathing exercises, or mindful movement.
- Honor your energy rhythms: align work at your peak and monitor early signs of mental fatigue.
- Create clear boundaries between work and rest.
- Treat recovery as part of your focus practice, not separate from it.

Remember: Recovery isn't a sign of weakness—it's a mark of wisdom. The quality of your focus is directly proportional to the quality of your rest.

Plan for Obstacles

Principle: Anticipate challenges to overcome them.

Why: The path to better focus is not a straight line—it's a journey with inevitable obstacles. People who use mental contrasting (anticipating challenges while planning solutions) are significantly more likely to succeed than those who rely on positive thinking alone. Success comes not from avoiding obstacles but from preparing for them.

Action:

- Use mental contrasting effectively: Visualize outcome, identify obstacles, and create tailored strategy.
- Develop contingency plans - create if-then plans for common focus challenges.
- Identify your personal focus kryptonite.
- Build systems to support you through difficult periods.

Remember: Obstacles aren't failures—they're opportunities to strengthen your focus system. When you prepare for challenges in advance, they become stepping stones rather than stumbling blocks.

Write It Down, Track Your Path

Principle: What gets written gets done; what gets measured gets improved.

Why: With your obstacles identified and strategies prepared, the next step is making your plan concrete and trackable. People who write down their goals are 40% more likely to achieve them. But the real power comes from combining written goals with progress tracking. When you document your journey, you not only create accountability but also gain insights into what works and what doesn't. Your mind can play tricks with memory—written records don't lie.

Action:

- *Document your focus journey:* 1. Write down your goals and obstacle-handling strategies. 2. Keep your written plans visible daily. 3. Update your strategies as you learn.
- *Track strategically:* 1. Monitor both quantitative and qualitative metrics. 2. Record which strategies work best for different challenges. 3. Note what enhances or diminishes your focus.
- *Review and adjust:* 1. Conduct regular progress checks. 2. Celebrate improvements. 3. Refine your approach based on data.

Remember: Your focus journey is too important to trust to memory alone. Writing creates commitment, tracking ensures progress, and regular review enables improvement. When you document your path, you transform vague intentions into measurable growth.

Focus Forward: Evolution and Legacy

As we conclude our journey together, let's appreciate how far we've come. Throughout this book, we've discovered that **enhancing cognitive performance**—whether through better habits, optimized environments, or physical and mental wellbeing—**naturally strengthens our ability to concentrate**. Each element we've explored contributes to building a stronger, more focused mind.

Above all, we've learned this fundamental truth: **a focused mind is a disciplined mind** – and in our days full of distractions, discipline becomes your anchor. It's not about having heroic willpower or perfect concentration—it's about building systems and habits that make focus your default state. Through consistent practice, what starts as conscious effort gradually becomes natural and automatic.

Yes, there will be days when your focus wavers, when distractions feel overwhelming, or when your energy isn't optimal. That's completely normal. What matters isn't the absence of struggles but how you respond to them. Remember that every small choice matters: each focused moment builds momentum, every mindful decision strengthens your practice, and all these tiny improvements multiply over time.

When you cultivate focus through discipline, you're not just enhancing your productivity—you're developing a capability that enriches every aspect of your life. **A focused mind is a rested mind, one that's nourished by good habits and healthy choices**. So, in our increasingly fragmented world, your ability to maintain focus becomes both your superpower and your legacy, inspiring those around you to discover their own capacity for sustained attention.

Your journey continues beyond these pages, offering new opportunities each day to apply these principles and refine your practice. The tools are in your hands—how will you use them?

Final Thoughts

As a neuroscientist who has struggled with focus, I understand firsthand how challenging it can be to maintain concentration, especially in today's world. But I've also learned something profound along the way: focus isn't just about getting more done – it's about living more intentionally. It's about being present for the moments that matter, creating work that matters, and building a life that reflects your values.

Remember, developing focus isn't about achieving perfection—it's about progress. The strategies shared in these pages are tools, not rules. Some may work better for you than others, and that's perfectly fine. After all, every expert was once a beginner, every master practice started with a single moment, and every focus journey begins with one conscious choice.

If there's one thing I hope you take away from this book, it's that improving your focus is absolutely possible. Your brain is remarkably adaptable, and with the right approach, you can train it to maintain better concentration. Take what resonates from these pages, adapt it to your life, and trust in the process of growth. The principles we've explored aren't just techniques; they're keys to unlocking a more mindful, productive, and purposeful way of living.

Start small, be patient with yourself, and celebrate your progress along the way. Your focus journey is uniquely yours, and it doesn't end with the closing of this book – it begins with your very next choice. The question isn't whether you can become a focus master – you absolutely can. The question is: what's the first small step you'll take on your journey?

I'd love to hear about your focus journey and any insights you've gained along the way. Feel free to reach out at: *ossama@focusedmindbook.com* – I read all messages and do my best to respond and help whenever I can!

Here's to your journey toward unwavering focus!

Warmly,

Ossama Khalaf

Your Focus Journey Continues

Your focus journey doesn't end here. I've created some helpful tools for you.

Please visit focusedmindbook.com/resources to access practical resources and templates that complement what you've learned in this book. You'll also find regularly updated articles and tips to help you along your focus journey.

Remember, each step in your focus journey matters. I hope these tools help support you along the way.

Connect with me on LinkedIn: @OssamaKhalaf

Acknowledgements

The journey of writing "Focused Mind" would not have been possible without standing on the shoulders of giants. I am deeply indebted to the pioneering researchers and authors whose work has illuminated our understanding of attention, focus, and productivity. Special gratitude goes to the groundbreaking studies from the fields of neuroscience, psychology, and behavioral science that form the foundation of this book.

My sincere appreciation extends to my mentors throughout my career. Your guidance has shaped not only my scientific thinking but also my approach to focus and productivity.

To my colleagues and fellow researchers who shared their insights and challenged my thinking – your contributions have been invaluable.

To all my mentees who trusted me with their struggles and triumphs in maintaining focus – your experiences have enriched this book immeasurably.

Finally, to my dear wife who supported me through this journey – your patience, encouragement, and understanding have made this work possible. You have been my anchor through the ups and downs of the writing process.

This book is a testament to the collective wisdom and support of all these individuals. While the words are mine, the insights belong to a community of thinkers, researchers, and supporters who have contributed to our understanding of how to harness the power of focus in an increasingly distracted world.

End Notes

Cognitive Tug-of-War

Corbetta, M., & Shulman, G. L. (2002). Control of goal-directed and stimulus-driven attention in the brain. Nature Reviews Neuroscience, 3(3), 201-215. This influential article reviews the two distinct yet interacting attentional systems – the dorsal and ventral attention networks (DAN and VAN) that we've covered in the book.

Shapeshifting Mind

Maguire, E. A., Gadian, D. G., Johnsrude, I. S., Good, C. D., Ashburner, J., Frackowiak, R. S., & Frith, C. D. (2000). Navigation-related structural change in the hippocampi of taxi drivers. Proceedings of the National Academy of Sciences, 97(8), 4398-4403. This groundbreaking study examined the brains of London taxi drivers using structural Magnetic Resonance Imaging (MRI). This study provided evidence for experience-dependent plasticity in the adult human brain.

Woollett, K., & Maguire, E. A. (2011). Acquiring "the Knowledge" of London's layout drives structural brain changes. Current Biology, 21(24), 2109-2114. This follow-up study examined London taxi drivers before and after they acquired "The Knowledge" - an intensive training program on London's layout. The study provided evidence for training-induced plasticity in the adult human brain, and that these structural changes can occur relatively quickly (over a few years). This is a powerful demonstration of how learning and experience can shape brain structure, even in adulthood.

Posner, M. I., & Rothbart, M. K. (2007). Research on attention networks as a model for the integration of psychological science. Annual Review of Psychology, 58, 1-23.

Tang, Y. Y., & Posner, M. I. (2009). Attention training and attention state training. Trends in cognitive sciences, 13(5), 222-227. This paper is significant for its discussion of different approaches to improving attention and their potential mechanisms.

Mrazek, M. D., Franklin, M. S., Phillips, D. T., Baird, B., & Schooler, J. W. (2013). Mindfulness training improves working memory capacity and GRE performance while reducing mind wandering. Psychological Science, 24(5), 776-781. This paper provides evidence for the cognitive benefits of short-term attention training (2-week program), particularly in educational contexts.

Takeuchi, H., Sekiguchi, A., Taki, Y., Yokoyama, S., Yomogida, Y., Komuro, N., ... & Kawashima, R. (2010). Training of working memory impacts structural connectivity. Journal of Neuroscience, 30(9), 3297-3303. This paper investigated the effects of working memory training on brain structure demonstrating that cognitive training can induce structural changes in the brain, providing evidence for training-induced plasticity in the adult brain.

Kühn, S., Gleich, T., Lorenz, R. C., Lindenberger, U., & Gallinat, J. (2014). Playing Super Mario induces structural brain plasticity: gray matter changes resulting from training with a commercial video game. Molecular Psychiatry, 19(2), 265-271. This study examined the effects of playing a video game on brain structure. The results show that engaging in complex spatial navigation and motor coordination tasks, even in the form of video games, can lead to structural brain changes. It highlights the potential of video games as cognitive training tools.

Focus Modulators

McNab, F., Varrone, A., Farde, L., Jucaite, A., Bystritsky, P., Forssberg, H., & Klingberg, T. (2009). Changes in cortical dopamine D1 receptor binding associated with cognitive training. Science, 323(5915), 800-802. This study demonstrates how working memory training can alter dopamine D1 receptor binding in the prefrontal cortex, linking cognitive training to changes in the dopamine system and improved cognitive performance.

Cools, R., & D'Esposito, M. (2011). Inverted-U-shaped dopamine actions on human working memory and cognitive control. Biological psychiatry, 69(12), e113-e125. This study describes how optimal levels of dopamine in the PFC are crucial for maintaining task-relevant information and ignoring distractors.

Sara, S. J., & Bouret, S. (2012). Orienting and reorienting: the locus coeruleus mediates cognition through arousal. Neuron, 76(1), 130-141. This review discusses how the locus coeruleus-norepinephrine system influences cognition through arousal, highlighting norepinephrine's role in attention and cognitive flexibility.

Sarter M, Gehring WJ, Kozak R. (2006). More attention must be paid: the neurobiology of attentional effort. Brain Research Reviews, 51(2):145-60. This paper reviews the neurobiology of attentional effort, focusing on the cholinergic system's role in sustained attention and cognitive control.

Sarter, M., Lustig, C., Berry, A. S., Gritton, H., Howe, W. M., & Parikh, V. (2016). What do phasic cholinergic signals do? Neurobiology of Learning and Memory, 130, 135-141. This study investigates the function of cholinergic signals in attention and cognitive processing, further elucidating acetylcholine's role in focus and learning.

Schmitt, J. A., Wingen, M., Ramaekers, J. G., Evers, E. A., & Riedel, W. J. (2006). Serotonin and human cognitive performance. Current Pharmaceutical Design, 12(20), 2473-2486. This review explores serotonin's effects on human cognitive performance, including its influence on attention, memory, and executive function.

Samardzic, J., Jadzic, D., Hencic, B., Jancic, J., & Strac, D. S. (2018). Introductory Chapter: GABA/Glutamate Balance: A Key for Normal Brain Functioning. New Developments in Neurotransmission Research. InTech. This book chapter discusses that maintaining the proper GABA/glutamate balance is crucial for optimal cognitive performance, including attention.

Internal Timekeeper

Richards, J., & Gumz, M. L. (2012). Advances in understanding the peripheral circadian clocks. FASEB (Federation of American Societies for Experimental Biology) journal, 26(9), 3602–3613. This review focuses on peripheral circadian clocks, which are relevant to understanding how circadian rhythms affect various bodily functions, including cognitive performance.

Cajochen, C. (2007). Alerting effects of light. Sleep Medicine Reviews, 11(6), 453-464. This review discusses how light exposure affects alertness, directly relating to how circadian rhythms influence attention and focus throughout the day.

Schmidt, C., Collette, F., Cajochen, C., & Peigneux, P. (2007). A time to think: Circadian rhythms in human cognition. Cognitive Neuropsychology, 24(7), 755-789. This review explores how circadian rhythms impact human cognition, including attention and executive functions, providing a comprehensive overview of the topic.

Lim, J., & Dinges, D. F. (2010). A meta-analysis of the impact of short-term sleep deprivation on cognitive variables. Psychological Bulletin, 136(3), 375-389. This meta-analysis examines how short-term sleep deprivation affects cognitive performance, including attention.

Goel, N., Basner, M., Rao, H., & Dinges, D. F. (2013). Circadian rhythms, sleep deprivation, and human performance. Progress in Molecular Biology and Translational Science, 119, 155-190. This is an extensive review of how circadian rhythms and sleep deprivation affect human performance, including attention and cognitive function.

Wehrens, S. M. T., Christou, S., Isherwood, C., Middleton, B., Gibbs, M. A., Archer, S. N., Skene, D. J., & Johnston, J. D. (2017). Meal Timing Regulates the Human Circadian System. Current biology, 27(12), 1768-1775. This study shows how meal timing can regulate the human circadian system, potentially affecting cognitive performance and attention.

Roenneberg, T., Wirz-Justice, A., & Merrow, M. (2003). Life between clocks: Daily temporal patterns of human chronotypes. Journal of Biological Rhythms, 18(1), 80-90. This paper introduces the concept of chronotypes, relevant to understanding individual differences in circadian rhythms and their impact on cognitive function.

Ehlers, C. L., Frank, E., & Kupfer, D. J. (1988). Social zeitgebers and biological rhythms: A unified approach to understanding the etiology of depression. Archives of General Psychiatry, 45(10), 948-952. This review introduces the concept of social zeitgebers, which can influence circadian rhythms. The review suggests that a disruption of social rhythms may result in instability in biological rhythms.

Gabriel, B. M., & Zierath, J. R. (2019). Circadian rhythms and exercise — re-setting the clock in metabolic disease. Nature Reviews Endocrinology, 15(4), 197-206. Focusing on exercise and metabolic disease, this review discusses how physical activity can reset circadian rhythms, potentially affecting cognitive performance.

Chang, A. M., Aeschbach, D., Duffy, J. F., & Czeisler, C. A. (2015). Evening use of light-emitting eReaders negatively affects sleep, circadian timing, and next-morning alertness. Proceedings of the National Academy of Sciences, 112(4), 1232-1237. This study demonstrates how evening use of light-emitting devices can disrupt circadian rhythms and next-morning alertness, directly affecting focus and attention.

Verwey, M., Dhir, S., & Amir, S. (2016). Circadian influences on dopamine circuits of the brain: regulation of striatal rhythms of clock gene expression and implications for psychopathology and disease. F1000Research, 5, F1000 Faculty Rev-2062. This review highlights the bidirectional relationship between circadian rhythms and dopamine: circadian rhythms influence dopamine release, while dopamine can also affect circadian rhythms.

Mind Mischief

Castellanos, F. X., Sonuga-Barke, E. J., Milham, M. P., & Tannock, R. (2006). Characterizing cognition in ADHD: beyond executive dysfunction. Trends in Cognitive Sciences, 10(3), 117-123. This paper is an important review article in the field of ADHD research. The article reviews the complexity of the disorder's cognitive profile.

Rock, P. L., Roiser, J. P., Riedel, W. J., & Blackwell, A. D. (2014). Cognitive impairment in depression: a systematic review and meta-analysis. Psychological Medicine, 44(10), 2029-2040. This paper is a comprehensive meta-analysis of 24 different cognitive tests across numerous studies. They report significant cognitive deficits in depression across various domains, including: executive function, memory, attention, and processing speed.

Eysenck, M. W., Derakshan, N., Santos, R., & Calvo, M. G. (2007). Anxiety and cognitive performance: Attentional control theory. Emotion, 7(2), 336-353. This paper explains the Attentional Control Theory (ACT) of anxiety. This paper offers a framework for understanding the mechanisms underlying anxiety's effects on cognitive performance, particularly attention and working memory.

Abramovitch, A., Abramowitz, J. S., & Mittelman, A. (2013). Neuropsychological investigations in obsessive–compulsive disorder: A systematic review of methodological challenges. Psychiatry Research, 210(1), 1-11. A comprehensive meta-analysis analyzing 115 studies comparing cognitive function in adults with OCD to healthy controls. It highlights the nature and extent of cognitive deficits in OCD.

Keehn, B., Müller, R. A., & Townsend, J. (2013). Atypical attentional networks and the emergence of autism. Neuroscience & Biobehavioral Reviews, 37(2), 164-183. This paper reviews research on attentional networks in individuals with Autism Spectrum Disorder (ASD). It integrates findings across multiple studies highlighting the role of attention in ASD.

Martínez-Arán, A., Vieta, E., Reinares, M., Colom, F., Torrent, C., Sánchez-Moreno, J., Benabarre, A., Goikolea, J.M., Comes, M., & Salamero, M. (2004). Cognitive function across manic or hypomanic, depressed, and euthymic states in bipolar disorder. American Journal of Psychiatry, 161(2), 262-270. This study examines the cognitive function in 108 patients of bipolar disorder across different mood states: manic/hypomanic, depressed, and euthymic (stable mood).

Snyder, H. R., et al. (2015). Using executive function theory to facilitate more targeted, individualized assessment of executive functions. Neuropsychology Review, 25(3), 284-303. The paper reviews evidence of Executive Function (EF) impairments across various psychopathologies, including ADHD, Anxiety, and Depression.

Distraction Overload

Killingsworth, M. A., & Gilbert, D. T. (2010). A wandering mind is an unhappy mind. Science (New York, N.Y.), 330(6006), 932. This study found that people's minds wander frequently, regardless of what they're doing, and can potentially impact a significant portion of their daily activities, including work tasks.

Mooneyham, B. W., & Schooler, J. W. (2013). The costs and benefits of mind-wandering: a review. Canadian journal of experimental, 67(1),

11–18. This review underscores the benefits of day-dreaming in enhancing creativity, but it also emphasizes that it can significantly impair performance on many tasks.

Alderson-Day, B., & Fernyhough, C. (2015). Inner Speech: Development, Cognitive Functions, Phenomenology, and Neurobiology. Psychological bulletin, 141(5), 931–965. This review explores the phenomenon of internal monologue in our heads, and highlights how it can often pull our attention away from tasks at hand.

Williamson, V. J., Liikkanen, L. A., Jakubowski, K., & Stewart, L. (2014). Sticky tunes: how do people react to involuntary musical imagery? PloS one, 9(1), e86170. This study highlights how common and potentially disruptive internal auditory distractions can be in our daily lives, including during work hours.

Hardman, C. A., Rogers, P. J., Etchells, K. A., Houstoun, K. V., & Munafò, M. R. (2013). The effects of food-related attentional bias training on appetite and food intake. Appetite, 71, 295–300. This study suggests that hunger can significantly impact our ability to focus on non-food-related tasks.

Szalma, J. L., & Hancock, P. A. (2011). Noise effects on human performance: a meta-analytic synthesis. Psychological bulletin, 137(4), 682–707. This study highlights how environmental noise, a common external distraction, can significantly impact work performance.

Forster, S., & Lavie, N. (2008). Attentional capture by entirely irrelevant distractors. Visual Cognition, 16(2-3), 200-214. This study is crucial for understanding how visual distractions in the workplace (e.g., movement, flashing lights) can involuntarily capture attention and disrupt focus.

MacKay, J. (2019). Screen time stats 2019: Here's how much you use your phone during the workday. RescueTime Blog. https://blog.rescuetime.com/screen-time-stats-2018/ This blog post provides insights into smartphone usage patterns during work hours, based on data from RescueTime's productivity software. It offers statistics on average screen time, frequency of phone checks, and the impact of digital distractions on workplace productivity.

Pielot, M., Church, K., & de Oliveira, R. (2014). An in-situ study of mobile phone notifications. In Proceedings of the 16th International Conference on Human-Computer Interaction with Mobile Devices & Services (pp. 233-242). ACM. This study examines the nature and frequency of mobile phone notifications in real-world settings. The researchers collected data on how often people receive notifications, how they respond to them, and the impact on attention and task interruption.

Screen Education. (2019). Digital Distraction in the Workplace. www.screeneducation.org/digital-distraction-in-the-workplace.html This report by Screen Education explores the prevalence and impact of digital distractions in professional environments. It presents data on how digital devices affect workplace productivity, employee focus, and overall job performance. The study offers insights into the challenges businesses face in managing digital distractions and potential strategies for mitigation.

Asurion. (2019). Americans check their phones 96 times a day. PR Newswire. While not a peer-reviewed study, this report provides insight into the frequency of potential tech-related distractions in daily life, which can significantly impact workplace focus.

Mark, G., Gudith, D., & Klocke, U. (2008). The cost of interrupted work: More speed and stress. Proceedings of the SIGCHI Conference on Human Factors in Computing Systems, 107-110. This research directly addresses the impact of interruptions on work performance and worker well-being.

Sykes, E. R. (2011). Interruptions in the workplace: A case study to reduce their effects. International Journal of Information Management, 31(4), 385-394. This case study investigates interruptions and their impact on productivity and work quality, also discusses strategies to reduce the effects of interruptions in the workplace.

Christiansen, J. (2022, November 1). Failure to Focus: Distractions are Killing Our Ability to Focus at Work and at Home | Crucial Learning. Crucial Learning. https://cruciallearning.com/press/failure-to-focus/ This article highlights a growing crisis in our ability to focus to do deep work or concentration on tasks for even short periods.

Bialowolski P, McNeely E, VanderWeele TJ, Weziak-Bialowolska D (2020) Ill health and distraction at work: Costs and drivers for productivity loss. PLOS ONE 15(3): e0230562. In this study, researchers looked at a diverse workforce of over 3,000 people, including both office and factory workers, and points out that workplace distractions as the main drain on productivity.

Spira, J. B., Feintuch, J. B., Basex, Inc., Goldes, D. M., & Spira, G. (2005). The Cost of Not Paying Attention: How Interruptions Impact Knowledge Worker Productivity (Basilio Alferow, Ed.). https://www.interruptions.net/literature/Spira-Basex05.pdf The report underscores the impact of interruptions on workplace productivity, particularly for knowledge workers. It provides concrete numbers on the time and financial costs of workplace distractions, which can be useful for understanding the scale of the issue.

Studienteam Vera Starker, Next Work Innnovation Think Tank, Roos, K., Dr., Bracht, E. M., Dr., Hanke, D. J., Graudenz, D., Coppik, R., Dr., Wissenschaftlicher Beirat, Busch, V., Prof. Dr., & Van Dick, R. (2022). Kosten von Arbeitsunterbrechungen für deutsche Unternehmen. Auswirkungen von Fragmentierung auf Produktivität und Stressentwicklung. This report in German conducted on the work habits of 637 people across 25 companies and 12 industries in Germany. It reports the costs big companies in Germany pay due to interruptions.

Csikszentmihalyi, M. (1990). Flow: The Psychology of Optimal Experience (First edition). Harper & Row. This book introduces the concept of "flow," a state of optimal experience characterized by deep concentration and enjoyment.

Mullainathan, S., & Shafir, E. (2013). Scarcity: Why having too little means so much. Macmillan. This book explores how scarcity of time affects cognitive capacity which is relevant to understanding the impact on focus and decision-making in daily life.

Leroy, S. (2009). Why is it so hard to do my work? The challenge of attention residue when switching between work tasks. Organizational Behavior and Human Decision Processes, 109(2), 168-181. This study examines "attention residue" when switching tasks. Found that thoughts about a previous task can reduce performance on the next task by up to 40%.

Foroughi, C. K., Werner, N. E., Nelson, E. T., & Boehm-Davis, D. A. (2014). Do interruptions affect quality of work? Human Factors, 56(7), 1262-1271. This study examined how interruptions affect work quality, particularly in complex cognitive tasks. The study highlights that even brief interruptions can have significant negative impacts on work quality, especially for complex cognitive tasks.

Altmann, E. M., Trafton, J. G., & Hambrick, D. Z. (2014). Momentary interruptions can derail the train of thought. Journal of Experimental Psychology: General, 143(1), 215-226. This study investigated the effects of brief interruptions on task performance. It demonstrated that even momentary interruptions can significantly disrupt cognitive processes and lead to errors, highlighting the importance of maintaining uninterrupted focus for complex tasks.

Speier, C., Valacich, J. S., & Vessey, I. (1999). The influence of task interruption on individual decision making: An information overload perspective. Decision Sciences, 30(2), 337-360. This research showed that interruptions can be particularly detrimental to performance on complex tasks or under high information load conditions.

Westbrook, J. I., Woods, A., Rob, M. I., Dunsmuir, W. T., & Day, R. O. (2010). Association of interruptions with an increased risk and severity of medication administration errors. Archives of Internal medicine,

170(8), 683-690. This research examines the impact of interruptions on medication administration errors in healthcare settings.

Habit Hurdles

Wood, W., & Rünger, D. (2016). Psychology of habit. Annual Review of Psychology, 67, 289-314. This review article provides an overview of the psychology of habits, including their formation and impact on daily behavior.

Duhigg, C. (2012). The Power of Habit: Why We Do What We Do in Life and Business. Random House. This book provides a comprehensive look at the science of habit formation and change.

Yin, H. H., & Knowlton, B. J. (2006). The role of the basal ganglia in habit formation. Nature Reviews Neuroscience, 7(6), 464-476. This review provides insights into how the basal ganglia interact with other brain regions to support habit formation.

Newport, C. (2016). Deep work: Rules for focused success in a distracted world. Grand Central Publishing. This book synthesizes research on the benefits of deep, focused work and provides strategies for implementing it.

Ophir, E., Nass, C., & Wagner, A. D. (2009). Cognitive control in media multitaskers. Proceedings of the National Academy of Sciences, 106(37), 15583-15587. This study found that heavy media multitaskers performed worse on cognitive control tasks compared to light media multitaskers. This suggests that the habit of focusing on single tasks (as in deep work) may improve cognitive control and concentration abilities.

Maza, M. T., Fox, K. A., Kwon, S., Flannery, J. E., Lindquist, K. A., Prinstein, M. J., & Telzer, E. H. (2023). Association of Habitual Checking Behaviors on Social Media With Longitudinal Functional Brain Development. JAMA Pediatrics, 177(2), 160. This study demonstrates how checking habits reshape brain's reward circuitry over time. They did a 3-year longitudinal study on more than 150 adolescents to find that habitual social media checking is associated with hyper-sensitivity to social feedback and numbness in reward processing.

Deshpande, T., Kate, S., Zunjar, V., Bhore, S., & Kenith, A. (2023, September 28). "Brain Behind The screen". This study reports the impact of social media use on "Happy Hormones." It shows that social media use can stimulate serotonin release and contribute to feelings of connection and social validation, but excessive use can lead to social comparison, cyberbullying, and feelings of inadequacy, which are associated with lowered serotonin levels and increased risk of mood disorders.

Marty-Dugas, J., Ralph, B. C. W., Oakman, J. M., & Smilek, D. (2018). The relation between smartphone use and everyday inattention. Psychology of Consciousness: Theory, Research, and Practice, 5(1), 46–62. This study reports that higher levels of smartphone use were associated with increased reports of everyday inattention. The study highlights that habitual smartphone use can lead to increased distraction and decreased attention in everyday life.

Oulasvirta, A., Rattenbury, T., Ma, L., & Raita, E. (2012). Habits make smartphone use more pervasive. Personal and Ubiquitous Computing, 16(1), 105-114. This study explored how habits can make smartphone use more automatic and frequent, potentially leading to increased distractions and interruptions in daily life.

Duke, É., & Montag, C. (2017). Smartphone addiction, daily interruptions and self-reported productivity. Addictive Behaviors Reports, 6, 90-95. This research underscores the potential negative impact of habitual smartphone use on productivity, particularly through increased interruptions.

Purvi, Chandrakar, Vishal, Singh., V., K., Verma., Pankaj, Pandey. (2024). Effects of Social Media on Brain Function. International Journal For Multidisciplinary Research. This study links specific digital behaviors to neurochemical changes, where it shows regular social media use affects dopamine baseline levels and receptor sensitivity.

Mandolesi, L., Polverino, A., Montuori, S., Foti, F., Ferraioli, G., Sorrentino, P., & Sorrentino, G. (2018). Effects of Physical Exercise on Cognitive Functioning and Wellbeing: Biological and Psychological Benefits. Frontiers in Psychology, 9, 509. This comprehensive review examines the positive effects of physical exercise on cognitive function and overall well-being. It highlights how regular physical activity can enhance various cognitive abilities, including memory and attention.

Basso, J. C., & Suzuki, W. A. (2017). The Effects of Acute Exercise on Mood, Cognition, Neurophysiology, and Neurochemical Pathways: A Review. Brain Plasticity, 2(2), 127-152. This review article explores the immediate and long-term effects of exercise on mood and cognitive function. It delves into the neurochemical changes that occur with exercise, explaining how these changes can lead to improved focus and mental well-being.

Chae, B., & Zhu, R. (2014). Environmental disorder leads to self-regulatory failure. Journal of Consumer Research, 40(6), 1203-1218. This study examines how physical disorder in one's environment can lead to decreased self-control and focus. It provides evidence for the impact of our physical surroundings on our cognitive abilities.

Król, M., & Zdonek, D. (2020). Social Media and Its Impact on Academic Performance. Sustainability, 12(20), 8451. This research explores the relationship between social media use and academic performance, including factors like attention span and productivity. It highlights the potential negative effects of excessive social media use on cognitive function.

Steel, P. (2007). The nature of procrastination: A meta-analytic and theoretical review of quintessential self-regulatory failure. Psychological Bulletin, 133(1), 65-94. This meta-analysis provides a comprehensive overview of procrastination research, offering a definition and exploring its nature and effects.

Ferrari, J. R., & Tice, D. M. (2000). Procrastination as a self-handicap for men and women: A task-avoidance strategy in a laboratory setting. Journal of Research in Personality, 34(1), 73-83. This study explores procrastination as a self-handicapping behavior, providing insights into why people procrastinate.

Tice, D. M., & Baumeister, R. F. (1997). Longitudinal study of procrastination, performance, stress, and health: The costs and benefits of dawdling. Psychological Science, 8(6), 454-458. This longitudinal study examines the effects of procrastination on academic performance, stress, and health. They found that students who procrastinated experienced more stress and illness and performed worse academically than non-procrastinators. The procrastinators did report less stress early in the semester, but they paid for it with high stress and poorer health later.

Gollwitzer, P. M. (1999). Implementation intentions: Strong effects of simple plans. American Psychologist, 54(7), 493-503. This paper discusses the concept of implementation intentions and goal pursuit, which is relevant to understanding how procrastination affects goal achievement.

Przybylski, A. K., Murayama, K., DeHaan, C. R., & Gladwell, V. (2013). Motivational, emotional, and behavioral correlates of fear of missing out. Computers in Human Behavior, 29(4), 1841-1848. This study examines the relationship between fear of missing out (FOMO) and social media engagement.

Bowman, L. L., Levine, L. E., Waite, B. M., & Gendron, M. (2010). Can students really multitask? An experimental study of instant messaging while reading. Computers & Education, 54(4), 927-931. This study examines the effects of multitasking on reading comprehension and efficiency.

Sana, F., Weston, T., & Cepeda, N. J. (2013). Laptop multitasking hinders classroom learning for both users and nearby peers. Computers & Education, 62, 24-31. This study is about multitasking in educational settings and its impact on learning. They found that students who multitasked during lectures had significantly lower comprehension of the material. Also, students sitting near multitaskers also performed worse, even if they weren't multitasking themselves. This study highlights the detrimental effects of multitasking not only on the individual but also on those in their immediate vicinity, emphasizing the far-reaching consequences of divided attention in learning environments.

Rubinstein, J. S., Meyer, D. E., & Evans, J. E. (2001). Executive control of cognitive processes in task switching. Journal of experimental psychology: human perception and performance, 27(4), 763. This study reports that there is a significant cognitive cost to switching between tasks, both in terms of time and accuracy.

Adler, R. F., & Benbunan-Fich, R. (2012). Juggling on a high wire: Multitasking effects on performance. International Journal of Human-Computer Studies, 70(2), 156-168. This study examines the effects of multitasking on performance efficiency (productivity) and performance effectiveness (accuracy).

Loh, K. K., & Kanai, R. (2014). Higher media multi-tasking activity is associated with smaller gray-matter density in the anterior cingulate cortex. PloS one, 9(9), e106698. This study investigates the relationship between media multitasking and brain structure.

Walker, M. P., Gossel, S., Zhu, W., & Zhang, C. (2019). The Sleep-Deprived Human Brain. Nature Reviews Neuroscience, 20(7), 384-401. This review examines the wide-ranging effects of sleep deprivation on various aspects of cognitive function. It provides insights into how chronic sleep issues can reshape brain function and structure over time.

Gwin, J. A., Leidy, H. J., Hasek, L. Y., & Betts, J. A. (2022). Eating before sleep and cognitive function: A narrative review. Advances in Nutrition, 13(5), 1756-1778. This review article explores the relationship between late-night eating and cognitive performance. It discusses how meal timing, especially eating close to bedtime, can affect sleep quality and next-day cognitive function.

Energy Drain

Pilcher, J. J., & Huffcutt, A. I. (1996). Effects of sleep deprivation on performance: A meta-analysis. Sleep, 19(4), 318-326. This meta-analysis demonstrates the significant negative effects of sleep deprivation on human performance, particularly in cognitive tasks, directly relating to how fatigue impacts concentration.

Lim, J., & Dinges, D. F. (2010). A meta-analysis of the impact of short-term sleep deprivation on cognitive variables. Psychological Bulletin, 136(3), 375-389. This meta-analysis demonstrates how sleep deprivation negatively affects various cognitive functions, particularly attention and working memory.

Marcora, S. M., Staiano, W., & Manning, V. (2009). Mental fatigue impairs physical performance in humans. Journal of Applied Physiology, 106(3), 857-864.This study shows the link between mental and physical fatigue, suggesting that cognitive exertion can lead to overall fatigue, affecting both mental and physical performance.

Van Cutsem, J., Marcora, S., De Pauw, K., Bailey, S., Meeusen, R., & Roelands, B. (2017). The effects of mental fatigue on physical performance: A systematic review. Sports Medicine, 47(8), 1569-1588. This systematic review explores how mental fatigue affects physical endurance and perception of effort, demonstrating the far-reaching effects of cognitive exhaustion.

Breymeyer, K. L., Lampe, J. W., McGregor, B. A., & Neuhouser, M. L. (2016). Subjective mood and energy levels of healthy weight and overweight/obese healthy adults on high-and low-glycemic load experimental diets. Appetite, 107, 253-259. This research reports that diets high in processed foods and sugar (which typically have a high glycemic load) can contribute to energy spikes and crashes, potentially leading to increased fatigue. The effects were consistent across both healthy weight and overweight/obese participants.

Jiao, L., Kern, D. M., & Chow, S. M. (2021). Fast food consumption and its associations with obesity, hypertension, and fatigue among United States Coast Guard active duty members. Obesity Science & Practice, 7(2), 197-204. This study examined the relationship between fast food consumption and various health outcomes, including fatigue, among active duty members of the United States Coast Guard. The study suggests that frequent fast food consumption may contribute to increased fatigue, potentially due to the nutritional composition of these meals.

O'Connor, P. J., & Puetz, T. W. (2005). Chronic physical activity and feelings of energy and fatigue. Medicine & Science in Sports & Exercise, 37(2), 299-305. This study examines the relationship between regular physical activity and subjective feelings of energy and fatigue. The study suggests that adopting a more active lifestyle can be an effective intervention for reducing fatigue.

Afari, N., & Buchwald, D. (2003). Chronic fatigue syndrome: A review. American Journal of Psychiatry, 160(2), 221-236. This review examines Chronic Fatigue Syndrome and its impact on daily functioning, highlighting how medical conditions can contribute to persistent fatigue affecting focus and productivity.

Boksem, M. A., Meijman, T. F., & Lorist, M. M. (2005). Effects of mental fatigue on attention: An ERP study. Cognitive Brain Research, 25(1), 107-116. This study demonstrates how mental fatigue impairs our ability to suppress irrelevant information, directly impacting our capacity to focus.

Moore, R. D., Romine, M. W., O'Connor, P. J., & Tomporowski, P. D. (2012). The influence of exercise-induced fatigue on cognitive function. Journal of Sports Sciences, 30(9), 841-850. This research explores how physical fatigue affects cognitive functions, particularly our ability to inhibit responses, which is crucial for maintaining focus.

Pattyn, N., Neyt, X., Henderickx, D., & Soetens, E. (2008). Psychophysiological investigation of vigilance decrement: Boredom or cognitive fatigue? Physiology & Behavior, 93(1-2), 369-378. This study investigates how fatigue alters our perception and processing of information, showing that tiredness can change not just our ability to focus, but how we interpret the world around us.

Åkerstedt, T., Knutsson, A., Westerholm, P., Theorell, T., Alfredsson, L., & Kecklund, G. (2002). Sleep disturbances, work stress and work hours: A cross-sectional study. Journal of Psychosomatic Research, 53(3), 741-748. This study highlights the strong relationship between stress and disturbed sleep, demonstrating how fatigue and stress can create a self-reinforcing cycle.

Kato, Y., Endo, H., & Kizuka, T. (2012). Mental fatigue and impaired response processes: Event-related brain potentials in a Go/NoGo task. International Journal of Psychophysiology, 85(1), 93-98. This research shows how chronic fatigue can alter our brain's response to stress, making us more susceptible to its effects and potentially impacting our ability to focus.

Minkel, J. D., Banks, S., Htaik, O., Moreta, M. C., Jones, C. W., McGlinchey, E. L., Simpson, N. S., & Dinges, D. F. (2012). Sleep deprivation and stressors: Evidence for elevated negative affect in response to mild stressors when sleep deprived. Emotion, 12(5), 1015-1020. The study demonstrates how fatigue (in this case, from sleep deprivation) can amplify our stress responses and increase anxiety levels, even in relatively benign situations. This heightened emotional reactivity can further impact our ability to focus and concentrate, illustrating the complex interplay between fatigue, stress, and cognitive function.

Stress Spiral

Gallup. (2017). State of the American Workplace. Gallup, Inc. This report provides statistics on workplace stress in America, offering insight into the prevalence of stress in professional environments.

Sadler, J., Cigna, Zaidi, A., The Wellbeing Project, & Fuller, S. (n.d.). 2019 CIGNA 360 WELL-BEING SURVEY. In WELL &BEYOND. https://munideporte.com/imagenes/documentacion/ficheros/0122EEB5.pdf. This study, known as the Cigna 360 Well-Being Survey, provides insights on the pervasive nature of work-related stress and its potential impact on focus and productivity worldwide.

Hunt, M. G., Marx, R., Lipson, C., & Young, J. (2018). No more FOMO: Limiting social media decreases loneliness and depression. Journal of Social and Clinical Psychology, 37(10), 751-768. This study examined how limiting social media use affects psychological well-being. Participants who limited social media use to 30 minutes per day showed significant reductions in loneliness, depression, and anxiety, along with improved concentration and reduced social comparison. The research provides compelling evidence for how social media consumption affects our mental bandwidth and ability to focus.

McEwen, B. S. (2007). Physiology and neurobiology of stress and adaptation: Central role of the brain. Physiological Reviews, 87(3), 873-904. This review examines the physiological and neurobiological effects of chronic stress, including its impact on brain structure and function.

Arnsten, A. F. T. (2009). Stress signalling pathways that impair prefrontal cortex structure and function. Nature Reviews Neuroscience, 10(6), 410-422. This review article discusses how chronic stress can lead to structural changes in the brain, particularly in areas responsible for attention and executive function.

Eysenck, M. W., Derakshan, N., Santos, R., & Calvo, M. G. (2007). Anxiety and cognitive performance: Attentional control theory. Emotion, 7(2), 336-353. This study introduces the Attentional Control Theory, explaining how anxiety impairs the efficiency of the central executive component of working memory, crucial for maintaining focus.

Malarkey, W. B., Pearl, D. K., Demers, L. M., Kiecolt-Glaser, J. K., & Glaser, R. (1995). Influence of academic stress and season on 24-hour mean concentrations of ACTH, cortisol, and β-endorphin. Psychoneuroendocrinology, 20(5), 499-508. This study investigates the physiological effects of academic stress, demonstrating how stress can lead to hormonal changes that affect cognitive function and physical well-being.

Keller, A., Litzelman, K., Wisk, L. E., Maddox, T., Cheng, E. R., Creswell, P. D., & Witt, W. P. (2012). Does the perception that stress affects health matter? The association with health and mortality. Health Psychology, 31(5), 677-684. This is an interesting study showing that stressing about stress or perceiving that you are under stress could be harmful in itself and can lead to negative health outcomes.

Schneiderman, N., Ironson, G., & Siegel, S. D. (2005). Stress and health: psychological, behavioral, and biological determinants. Annual Review of Clinical Psychology, 1, 607-628. This review article explores the intricate relationships between psychological stress and physical health, highlighting how stress can lead to various physical symptoms and create feedback loops.

Jamieson, J. P., Mendes, W. B., Blackstock, E., & Schmader, T. (2010). Turning the knots in your stomach into bows: Reappraising arousal improves performance on the GRE. Journal of Experimental Social Psychology, 46(1), 208-212. This study demonstrates how reframing our perception of stress can lead to improved performance under pressure. It highlights the power of mindset in managing stress and its effects on cognitive function.

Emotion Shift

Barrett, L. F. (2017). How emotions are made: The secret life of the brain. Houghton Mifflin Harcourt. This book presents how emotions are constructed, and provides insights into the relationship between emotions and cognitive processes.

Ekman, P. (1992). An argument for basic emotions. Cognition & Emotion, 6(3-4), 169-200. This seminal paper provides a foundation for understanding the nature of emotions and their impact on behavior and cognition.

Fredrickson, B. L. (2001). The role of positive emotions in positive psychology: The broaden-and-build theory of positive emotions. American Psychologist, 56(3), 218-226. This article explains how positive emotions can expand cognitive and behavioral repertoires.

Isen, A. M., Daubman, K. A., & Nowicki, G. P. (1987). Positive affect facilitates creative problem solving. Journal of Personality and Social Psychology, 52(6), 1122-1131. This study demonstrates how positive affect can enhance creative problem-solving abilities.

Ashby, F. G., Isen, A. M., & Turken, A. U. (1999). A neuropsychological theory of positive affect and its influence on cognition. Psychological Review, 106(3), 529-550. This paper explains how positive affect influences cognition, particularly cognitive flexibility and creative problem solving.

Derakshan, N., & Eysenck, M. W. (2010). Introduction to the special issue: Emotional states, attention, and working memory. Cognition and Emotion, 24(2), 189-199. This article discusses the relationships between emotional states, attention, and working memory.

Eysenck, M. W., Derakshan, N., Santos, R., & Calvo, M. G. (2007). Anxiety and cognitive performance: Attentional control theory. Emotion,

7(2), 336-353. This paper explains how anxiety impairs the efficiency of the central component of working memory and affects cognitive performance.

Grupe, D. W., & Nitschke, J. B. (2013). Uncertainty and anticipation in anxiety: An integrated neurobiological and psychological perspective. Nature Reviews Neuroscience, 14(7), 488-501. This review focuses on how uncertainty and anticipation contribute to anxiety and its effects on cognitive processes.

Chepenik, L. G., Cornew, L. A., & Farah, M. J. (2007). The influence of sad mood on cognition. Emotion, 7(4), 802-811. This study examines how sad mood influences various cognitive processes, including memory and attention. It provides evidence for the impact of even mild sadness on cognitive function.

Potegal, M., & Stemmler, G. (2010). Cross-disciplinary views of anger: Consensus and controversy. In M. Potegal, G. Stemmler, & C. Spielberger (Eds.), International Handbook of Anger (pp. 3-7). Springer. This book chapter offers a comprehensive overview of anger from various disciplinary perspectives, including its effects on cognition and behavior. It provides context for understanding anger as an "approach-related" emotion.

Eastwood, J. D., Frischen, A., Fenske, M. J., & Smilek, D. (2012). The Unengaged Mind: Defining Boredom in Terms of Attention. Perspectives on Psychological Science, 7(5), 482-495. This paper provides a comprehensive definition of boredom in terms of attention and engagement, offering insights into how boredom affects cognitive processes.

Danckert, J., & Merrifield, C. (2018). Boredom, sustained attention and the default mode network. Experimental Brain Research, 236(9), 2507-2518. This study explores the relationship between boredom, sustained attention, and brain activity, suggesting that boredom might serve an adaptive function in signaling the need for more engaging activities.

Focus 101

Locke, E. A., & Latham, G. P. (2019). The development of goal setting theory: A half century retrospective. Motivation Science, 5(2), 93-105. This landmark 50-year review of goal-setting research demonstrates clear link between specific goals and enhanced performance showing how clear goals improve focus and task engagement. The conclusion of this empirical research is that specific, challenging goals lead to better performance than vague "do your best" goals.

Robison, M. K., Unsworth, N., & Brewer, G. A. (2021). Examining the effects of goal-setting, feedback, and incentives on sustained attention. Journal of Experimental Psychology: Human Perception and Performance, 47(2), 208-226. This article reports that goal-setting, particularly specific and difficult goals, enhances focus duration especially when combined with feedback, which increases task engagement.

Chun, Y. H., & Rainey, H. G. (2005). Goal ambiguity and organizational performance in U.S. federal agencies. Journal of Public Administration Research and Theory, 15(4), 529-557. This research demonstrates how goal ambiguity affects focus and productivity. It shows that goal clarity directly correlates with improved performance and better focus.

Schweitzer, D., Baumeister, R. F., Laakso, E., & Ting, J. (2023). Self-control, limited willpower and decision fatigue in healthcare settings. Internal Medicine Journal, 53(1), 21-28. This research studies willpower depletion in professional settings showing why habits are more reliable and that it outperforms willpower for sustained performance.

Full Body Overhaul

Raichle, M. E., & Gusnard, D. A. (2002). Appraising the brain's energy budget. Proceedings of the National Academy of Sciences, 99(16), 10237-10239. This study explores how our brain manages and uses energy, revealing surprising insights about mental performance.

Ratey, J. J., & Hagerman, E. (2013). Spark: The revolutionary new science of exercise and the brain. Little, Brown and Company. A fascinating exploration of how physical activity transforms our brain for better thinking, learning, and emotional well-being.

Galbete, C., Toledo, E., Toledo, J. B., Bes-Rastrollo, M., Buil-Cosiales, P., Marti, A., Guillén-Grima, F., & Martínez-González, M. A. (2015). Mediterranean diet and cognitive function: The SUN project. Journal of Nutrition, Health & Aging, 19(3), 305-312. Research demonstrating the powerful link and long-term benefits between certain dietary patterns and brain health.

Adan, A. (2012). Cognitive performance and dehydration. Journal of the American College of Nutrition, 31(2), 71-78. An eye-opening look at how even mild dehydration can impact our thinking and concentration.

Riebl, S. K., & Davy, B. M. (2013). The hydration equation: Update on water balance and cognitive performance. ACSM's Health & Fitness Journal, 17(6), 21-28. A comprehensive review explaining the crucial relationship between hydration and mental performance.

Kohyama, J. (2021). Which is more important for health: Sleep quantity or sleep quality? Children, 8(7), 542. An insightful investigation into the relative importance of sleep duration versus sleep quality.

Lovato, N., & Lack, L. (2010). The effects of napping on cognitive functioning. Progress in Brain Research, 185, 155-166. A detailed look at how strategic napping can enhance mental performance.

Felice, F., Medori, S., & Macri, M. (2023). Move your body, boost your brain: The positive impact of physical activity on cognition across all age groups. Advances in Cardiovascular Diseases, 1(1), 1-10. The review highlights that physical activity (PA) has significant positive effects on cognitive functions such as attention, memory, and executive functions across all age groups. It emphasizes that both acute and chronic PA can induce beneficial changes in brain activation and cognitive performance.

Mazur, K., & Bulski, J. (2024). Effects of physical activity on cognitive function according to the latest selected scientific studies. Medical Science Pulse, 18(1), 2-8. A current review examining literature on physical activity's effects on cognitive functions, finding PA improves brain health, attention, and academic performance, and slows cognitive impairment.

Tyler, J., Podaras, M., Richardson, B. J., Roeder, N. M., Hammond, N., Hamilton, J., Blum, K., Gold, M. S., Baron, D. A., & Thanos, P. K. (2023). High intensity interval training exercise increases dopamine D2 levels and modulates brain dopamine signaling. Frontiers in Public Health, 11, 1123656. Cutting-edge research revealing how high-intensity exercise affects our brain's reward and pleasure systems.

Roig, M., & Cristini, J. (2024). Does dopamine mediate the effects of exercise on cognition? Journal of Physiology, 602(2), 427-428. An exploration of how exercise-induced dopamine release might enhance our cognitive abilities.

Fernández-Rodríguez, R., Álvarez-Bueno, C., Martínez-Ortega, I. A., Martínez-Vizcaíno, V., Mesas, A. E., & Notario-Pacheco, B. (2021). Immediate effect of high-intensity exercise on brain-derived neurotrophic factor in healthy young adults: A systematic review and meta-analysis. Journal of Sport and Health Science, 11(3), 367-375. A comprehensive analysis of how intense exercise immediately boosts brain-growth factors.

Huang, T. Y., Chen, F. T., Li, R. H., Hillman, C. H., Cline, T. L., Chu, C. H., Hung, T. M., & Chang, Y. K. (2022). Effects of acute resistance exercise on executive function: A systematic review of the moderating role of intensity and executive function domain. Sports Medicine - Open, 8(1), 1-17. Research showing how different intensities of strength training affect various aspects of thinking and decision-making.

Davidson, R. J., Kaliman, P., & Waugh, C. E. (2019). The neuroscience of resilience. Nature Reviews Neuroscience, 20(4), 227-242. An exploration of how our brains adapt and become more resilient through various practices.

Sukh, P., & Sharma, B. (2023). Application of meditation for stress management. International Journal of Yogic, Human Movement and Sports Sciences, 8(1), 44-47. Practical insights into how meditation can be used to manage daily stress.

Tang, Y. Y., Ma, Y., Wang, J., Fan, Y., Feng, S., Lu, Q., Yu, Q., Sui, D., Rothbart, M. K., Fan, M., & Posner, M. I. (2007). Short-term meditation training improves attention and self-regulation. Proceedings of the National Academy of Sciences, 104(43), 17152-17156. Evidence showing how even brief meditation practice can enhance focus and self-control.

Toussaint, L., Nguyen, Q. A., Roettger, C., Dixon, K., Offenbächer, M., Kohls, N., Hirsch, J. K., & Sirois, F. M. (2021). Effectiveness of progressive muscle relaxation, deep breathing, and guided imagery in promoting psychological and physiological states of relaxation. Evidence-Based Complementary and Alternative Medicine, 2021, 5924040. A comprehensive look at different relaxation techniques and their effectiveness.

Abdelfatah, D. A., Ahmed, D. A., Amer, M. A., Harby, S. S., & Abdelaty, H. I. (2024). The effect of deep breathing exercise versus 4-7-8 breathing technique on insomnia, pain, and anxiety among patients with burn injuries. Egyptian Journal of Nursing and Health Sciences, 4(1), 1-15. Research comparing different breathing techniques for managing sleep and anxiety.

Balban, M. Y., Neri, E., Kogon, M. M., Weed, L., Nouriani, B., Jo, B., Holl, G., Zeitzer, J. M., Spiegel, D., & Huberman, A. D. (2023). Brief structured respiration practices enhance mood and reduce physiological arousal. Cell Reports Medicine, 4(2), 100895. Recent findings on how structured breathing exercises can quickly improve our emotional state.

Knights, J. (2024). The power of emotional intelligence (managing emotions). International Journal of Emotional Intelligence, 15(1), 1-12. Current perspectives on using emotional intelligence in managing emotions rather than suppressing them, and using emotional awareness to guide thinking and actions, which can enhance focus and productivity.

Choudhury, K. (2013). Managing workplace stress: The cognitive behavioural way. Springer India. Practical strategies for handling work-related stress using cognitive-behavioral approaches, and emerge calmer, happier, and more confident.

Chen, B. (2023). Reframing the individual stress response. Journal of Stress Management, 31(2), 145-159. Modern insights into understanding the effects of reframing to manage our personal stress responses.

Jamieson, J. P., Mendes, W. B., Blackstock, E., & Schmader, T. (2010). Turning the knots in your stomach into bows: Reappraising arousal improves performance on the GRE. Journal of Experimental Social Psychology, 46(1), 208-212. This study demonstrates how reframing our perception of stress can lead to improved performance under pressure.

Focus Feng Shui

Rizky, Y. A., Khuzaini, K., & Shadiq, S. (2023). Decluttering for enhanced workplace performance: The 5S solution. Jurnal Inovasi Ekonomi, 8(02), 69-82. This article reports that excessive clutter creates a disorganized and distracting workspace increasing stress levels by elevating cortisol, which the brain interprets as a sign of failure. This heightened stress reduces cognitive abilities, ultimately hindering individual focus and productivity.

Vredeveldt, A., & Perfect, T. J. (2014). Reduction of environmental distraction to facilitate cognitive performance. Frontiers in Psychology, 5, 860. Research revealing how minimizing environmental distractions can enhance mental performance.

Clements-Croome, D. J. (2003). Environmental quality and the productive workplace. Building Services Journal, 25(3), 38-43. An exploration of how workplace environment directly impacts productivity and well-being.

Ferrari, J. R., Roster, C. A., Crum, K. P., & Pardo, M. A. (2018). Procrastinators and clutter: An ecological view of living with excessive "stuff". Current Psychology, 37(2), 441-444. A fascinating study on the relationship between clutter and procrastination.

Kastner, S., & Ungerleider, L. G. (2001). The neural basis of biased competition in human visual cortex. Neuropsychologia, 39(12), 1263-1276. Research into how our brains process visual information and handle distractions.

Adithya, G. A., Lenka, A., & Aslam, F. (2024). "Focus Flow" An approach to distraction free environment. International Journal of Innovative Research in Information Security, 11(1), 1-8. The paper emphasizes that a distraction-free environment, significantly enhances concentration by minimizing interruptions from external sources, thereby fostering a conducive atmosphere for productivity and effective task management.

Singh, M., Saini, M., Surjey, A., & Kate, V. (2023). Clean and organized desk helps improve your productivity. International Journal of Research Publication and Reviews, 4(4), 1440-1441. Evidence-based research on the impact of desk organization on work efficiency.

Nieuwenhuis, M., Knight, C., Postmes, T., & Haslam, S. A. (2014). The relative benefits of green versus lean office space: Three field experiments. Journal of Experimental Psychology: Applied, 20(3), 199-214. This study demonstrated increase in productivity in presence of office plants.

Lee, M., Lee, J., Park, B., & Miyazaki, Y. (2015). Nature-based intervention to reduce stress and improve cognitive function. Public Health, 129(11), 1427-1437. Research showing how exposure to plants reduces mental fatigue and enhances attention.

Mangen, A., & Velay, J. L. (2010). Digitizing literacy: Reflections on the haptics of writing. Advances in Haptics, 385-401. An insightful examination of how different writing methods affect cognitive processing.

Van Der Weel, F. R., & Van Der Meer, A. L. H. (2024). Handwriting but not typewriting leads to widespread brain connectivity: a high-density EEG study with implications for the classroom. Frontiers in Psychology, 14, 1123656. Groundbreaking research showing how handwriting activates neural networks differently than typing.

Mueller, P. A., & Oppenheimer, D. M. (2014). The pen is mightier than the keyboard: Advantages of longhand over laptop note taking. Psychological Science, 25(6), 1159-1168. Evidence supporting the cognitive benefits of handwritten notes versus typed ones.

Hedge, A., & Ray, E. J. (2004). Effects of an electronic height-adjustable worksurface on computer worker musculoskeletal discomfort and productivity. Human Factors and Ergonomics Society Annual Meeting, 48(8), 1091-1095. Research on how adjustable workstations can improve both comfort and productivity.

European Agency for Safety and Health at Work. (2017, September 2). Ergonomics in office work. OSHwiki. Comprehensive guide to implementing ergonomic principles in office environments.

U.S. Department of Labor & Occupational Safety and Health Administration. (2000). Ergonomics: The study of work. Authoritative resource on workplace ergonomics and its impact on employee well-being.

Robertson, M. M., Ciriello, V. M., & Garabet, A. M. (2012). Office ergonomics training and a sit-stand workstation: Effects on musculoskeletal and visual symptoms and performance of office workers. Applied Ergonomics, 44(1), 73-85. Comprehensive study on the benefits of ergonomic interventions in the workplace.

Robertson, M. M., Huang, Y. H., & Lee, J. (2017). Improvements in musculoskeletal health and computing behaviors: Effects of a macroergonomics office workplace and training intervention. Applied Ergonomics, 62, 182-196. Evidence of how ergonomic training can improve workplace health and productivity.

A. K. C., A., Albert, W. J., M. C. L., M., C. D., C., & Cardoso, M. R. (2024). Effects of implementing an active sitting protocol compared to using a traditional office chair and standing workstation. International Journal of Industrial Ergonomics, 101, 103587. Recent research comparing different sitting and standing arrangements.

Chandrasekaran, B., Pesola, A. J., Rao, C. R., & Arumugam, A. (2021). Does breaking up prolonged sitting improve cognitive functions in sedentary adults? BMC Musculoskeletal Disorders, 22(1), 274. Investigation into how movement breaks affect cognitive performance.

Tuckwell, G. A., Vincent, G. E., Gupta, C. C., & Ferguson, S. A. (2022). Does breaking up sitting in office-based settings result in cognitive performance improvements? Industrial Health, 60(6), 501-513. Analysis of how movement breaks impact cognitive function throughout the workday.

Garrett, G., Benden, M., Mehta, R., Pickens, A., Peres, S. C., & Zhao, H. (2016). Call center productivity over 6 months following a standing desk intervention. IIE Transactions on Occupational Ergonomics and Human Factors, 4(2-3), 188-195. Long-term study showing productivity improvements with standing desk implementation.

Pronk, N. P., Katz, A. S., Lowry, M., & Payfer, J. R. (2012). Reducing occupational sitting time and improving worker health: The Take-a-Stand Project. Preventing Chronic Disease, 9, E154. Comprehensive project demonstrating benefits of reduced sitting time.

Edwardson, C. L., Yates, T., Biddle, S. J. H., et al. (2018). Effectiveness of the Stand More AT (SMArT) Work intervention: cluster randomised controlled trial. BMJ, 363, k3870. Large-scale study on the effectiveness of standing desk interventions.

Caron, E. E., Marusich, L. R., Bakdash, J. Z., et al. (2022). The influence of posture on attention. Experimental Psychology, 69(6), 295-307. Research exploring how different postures affect attention and focus.

Talens-Estarelles, C., Cerviño, A., García-Lázaro, S., et al. (2023). The effects of breaks on digital eye strain, dry eye and binocular vision: Testing the 20-20-20 rule. Contact Lens & Anterior Eye, 46(2), 101744. Evidence supporting the effectiveness of structured screen breaks.

Chauhan, H., Jang, Y., Pradhan, S., & Moon, H. (2023). Personalized optimal room temperature and illuminance for maximizing occupant's mental task performance using physiological data. Journal of Building Engineering, 78, 107757. Research on optimal environmental conditions for cognitive performance.

eLife Sciences Publications Limited. (2024, April 23). Higher light levels may improve cognitive performance. eLife. Recent findings on how light intensity affects mental performance and productivity.

Son, S., Lamp, S., Yeom, D. J., & Sharp, N. (2024). The influence of lighting and thermal environments on sleep and cognitive function in older adults. Building and Environment, 265, 112028. Study examining how environmental factors affect cognition.

Golmohammadi, R., Yousefi, H., Safarpour Khotbesara, N., et al. (2021). Effects of light on attention and reaction time: A systematic review. Journal of Research in Health Sciences, 21(4), e00529. Comprehensive review of how lighting affects cognitive performance.

Chellappa, S. L., Gordijn, M. C., & Cajochen, C. (2011). Can light make us bright? Effects of light on cognition and sleep. Progress in Brain Research, 190, 119-133. Investigation into the relationship between light exposure and cognitive function.

Boubekri, M., Cheung, I. N., Reid, K. J., Wang, C., & Zee, P. C. (2014). Impact of windows and daylight exposure on overall health and sleep quality of office workers. Journal of Clinical Sleep Medicine, 10(06), 603-611. Research highlighting the importance of natural light for workplace well-being.

Hawes, B. K., Brunyé, T. T., Mahoney, C. R., Sullivan, J. M., & Aall, C. D. (2011). Effects of four workplace lighting technologies on perception, cognition and affective state. International Journal of Industrial Ergonomics, 42(1), 122-128. Study comparing different lighting solutions' impact on workplace performance.

De Kort, Y., & Smolders, K. (2010). Effects of dynamic lighting on office workers: First results of a field study with monthly alternating settings. Lighting Research & Technology, 42(3), 345-360. Investigation into how dynamic lighting affects workplace performance.

Bai, Y., Yu, S., & Liu, L. (2023). Effects of light transitions on comfort, mood, and cognitive performance at different temperatures: A strategy to design for indoor dynamic lighting. Building and Environment, 238, 109958. Research on optimizing lighting conditions for workplace comfort and performance.

Zhang, R., Campanella, C., Aristizabal, S., et al. (2020). Impacts of dynamic LED lighting on the well-being and experience of office occupants. International Journal of Environmental Research and Public Health, 17(19), 7217. Study examining how LED lighting affects workplace well-being.

Wurtman, R. J. (1975). The effects of light on the human body. Scientific American, 233(1), 69-77. Classic study on how light affects human physiology and performance.

Zaglauer, M. (2024). Akustisch optimierte Arbeitswelten. ASU Arbeitsmedizin Sozialmedizin Umweltmedizin, 59(10), 576-580. Research on optimizing workplace acoustics for better performance.

Michaud, A., & INCE. (2014). Silence is golden: Optimizing the acoustic environment. Tom Barrow Company Technical Report, 1-12. Practical guide to creating optimal acoustic environments for workplace productivity.

Mehta, R., Zhu, R., & Cheema, A. (2012). Is noise always bad? Exploring the effects of ambient noise on creative cognition. Journal of Consumer Research, 39(4), 784-799. Fascinating study on how different noise levels affect creativity.

World Health Organization. (2010, April 27). Noise. WHO Regional Office for Europe. Authoritative overview of noise impacts on human health and cognitive function.

Hongisto, V. (2008). Effects of sound masking on workers - a case study in a landscaped office. Proceedings of Acoustics, 08, 537-542. Investigation into sound masking techniques in open offices.

Cockerham, D., Lin, L., Chang, Z., & Schellen, M. (2018). Cross-sectional studies investigating the impacts of background sounds on cognitive task performance. In Educational Communications and Technology: Issues and Innovations (pp. 177-194). Springer. Research examining how different types of background noise affect cognitive performance.

Society for Human Resource Management. (2023, December 21). Too hot! Too cold! Temperature affects productivity. SHRM. Recent analysis of how temperature variations impact workplace productivity and employee comfort.

Hedge, A., & Gaygen, D. E. (2010). Indoor environment conditions and computer work in an office. HVAC&R Research, 16(2), 123-138. Study on how indoor environmental conditions affect computer work.

Seppänen, O., Fisk, W. J., & Lei, Q. H. (2006). Effect of temperature on task performance in office environment. Lawrence Berkeley National Laboratory Technical Report. Comprehensive analysis of temperature's impact on workplace performance.

Allen, J. G., MacNaughton, P., Satish, U., et al. (2015). Associations of cognitive function scores with carbon dioxide, ventilation, and volatile organic compound exposures in office workers. Environmental Health

Perspectives, 124(6), 805-812. Research on how air quality affects cognitive performance.

Mark, G., Iqbal, S., & Czerwinski, M. (2017). How blocking distractions affects workplace focus and productivity. ACM CHI Conference on Human Factors in Computing Systems, 2017, 5759-5771. Study on managing workplace distractions for better productivity.

Patterson, R. E. (2012). Cognitive engineering, cognitive augmentation, and information display. Journal of the Society for Information Display, 20(4), 208-213. Research on optimizing information display for cognitive performance.

FOCUS ROADMAP

Khalaf, O. (2023, May 11). The writing rituals of a Nobel Laureate: Insights from a literary icon. The Shortform. A concise exploration of Nobel Laureate Naguib Mahfouz's disciplined writing routine, highlighting how structured habits and dedicated time blocks contributed to his prolific literary output.

Oettingen, G., & Wadden, T. A. (1991). Expectation, fantasy, and weight loss: Is the impact of positive thinking always positive? Cognitive Therapy and Research, 15(2), 167-175. The original research paper introducing mental contrasting, demonstrating how combining positive fantasies with reality awareness leads to better outcomes than positive thinking alone.

Oettingen, G. (2015). Rethinking positive thinking: Inside the new science of motivation. This book challenges traditional views about positive thinking and introduces evidence-based approaches to goal achievement, including mental contrasting and implementation intentions.

IONOS. (2023, September 14). WOOP method: How to achieve goals more effectively. IONOS Digital Guide. A practical guide explaining the

WOOP (Wish, Outcome, Obstacle, Plan) method for goal achievement, based on Oettingen's research on mental contrasting.

Matthews, G. (2007). The impact of commitment, accountability, and written goals on goal achievement. Dominican University of California Psychology Faculty Presentations. https://scholar.dominican.edu/psychology-faculty-conference-presentations/3. This study of 149 professionals revealed that writing goals, making public commitments, and sharing regular progress reports dramatically increases goal achievement. Participants who implemented these strategies consistently outperformed those with unwritten or privately maintained goals.

Bandura, A. (1997). Self-efficacy: The exercise of control. W.H. Freeman and Company. This book established the foundation for understanding self-efficacy's role in personal development. In this seminal work, psychologist Albert Bandura explores how our beliefs about our capabilities influence our behavior and success. He demonstrates that self-efficacy—our belief in our ability to succeed at specific tasks—can be built through small, successful experiences, making it easier to tackle progressively bigger challenges.

Maltz, M. (1960). Psycho-cybernetics: A new way to get more living out of life. Prentice-Hall. This work introduced the concept of a structured timeframe for habit formation, based on Dr. Maltz's observations of his plastic surgery patients adapting to new appearances. While its 21-day timeline became popular wisdom, it paved the way for more detailed research into how habits actually form over time.

FOCUS COMMANDMENTS

Wilson, T. D., Reinhard, D. A., Westgate, E. C., Gilbert, D. T., Ellerbeck, N., Hahn, C., Brown, C. L., & Shaked, A. (2014). Just think: The challenges of the disengaged mind. Science, 345(6192), 75-77. A groundbreaking study revealing people's difficulty in spending time alone with their thoughts and the importance of developing this capacity.

Lemonick, M. (2014, July 3). Being alone with your thoughts. Time Magazine. Examines research on why people find it challenging to be alone with their thoughts and seem to prefer to be doing something rather than nothing, even if that something is negative.

Hunt, M. G., Marx, R., Lipson, C., & Young, J. (2018). No more FOMO: Limiting social media decreases loneliness and depression. Journal of Social and Clinical Psychology, 37(10), 751-768. This study provides compelling evidence for how social media consumption affects our mental bandwidth and ability to focus.

About the author

Ossama Khalaf is a neuroscientist whose journey into understanding the mysteries of the human brain began unexpectedly. After being trained as a pharmacist, his fascination with the wonders of the brain led him to pursue advanced studies in brain research, culminating in a PhD from Switzerland's prestigious Brain Mind Institute at École Polytechnique Fédérale de Lausanne (EPFL).

His unique research journey, spanning six countries across four continents, brought both rich scientific insights and personal challenges. Like many in today's fast-paced world, Ossama experienced firsthand the struggle to maintain focus and productivity amid constant change. These challenges inspired him to apply his scientific expertise to understand the mechanisms of attention and concentration, transforming personal obstacles into professional insights.

Drawing from both his rigorous research background and extensive mentoring experience, Ossama bridges the gap between complex neuroscience and practical, actionable strategies. His approach combines evidence-based methods with field-tested techniques that have helped numerous people enhance their focus and productivity. Through this book, he offers readers not just a scientific understanding of concentration, but a practical pathway to developing unwavering focus in pursuit of their goals.

When not investigating the neuroscience of attention, Ossama is passionate about helping others navigate the challenges of maintaining focus in our increasingly distracted world. His vision extends beyond individual transformation to fostering a community of focused, goal-oriented individuals equipped to thrive in today's demanding environment.

To continue learning about focus and productivity, please connect with Ossama to follow his insights on LinkedIn (@OssamaKhalaf), or join his community on Instagram (@focusedmind.book).

Made in United States
North Haven, CT
07 March 2026

89519606R00143